Holy FEAR

Fam
Fra

1479

Holy FEAR

A Christian Family's Walk in These Troubled Times

BOB FRALEY

CLP

ISBN —0-9612999-1-6

Published by
Christian Life Services
6438 East Jenan Drive
Scottsdale, Arizona 85254
Printed in the United States of America

ACKNOWLEDGEMENTS

Special appreciation is due Dr. Paul Knepper, Ph.D. for the many relentless hours he contributed in editing the manuscript as an act of friendship and as a labor of love to the Lord.

Also a word of thank you is due Mary Prether, Pat O'Shell and Edna Whicker for their excellent help and support in proofreading the manuscript.

Contents

PREFACE

Holy Fear presents the Christian's survival guide to living the normal Christian life in America during the last days. It is an account of how the Lord worked through our family, and specifically, how He guided the lives of my wife Barbara and me. This is not a theological presentation; I am not a theologian. It is a living word—something the Lord burned into our hearts beginning in the early 1970s. You will read the testimony of our family, and through what the Lord has revealed about the end times, you will receive practical instruction on living victoriously during the troubled times ahead.

In an earlier book entitled *The Last Days in America* (1984), I wrote about the United States in Bible prophecy. That book underscored the fact that American society as we know it is in its final hour. Our debt-ridden, morally-bankrupt society will be shaken by the Lord as never before. This book continues the *Last Days* theme. In *Holy Fear,* my purpose is to provide further prophetic insights into our spiritual Enemy's last-days battle plan; to make Christians aware of the danger of spiritual warfare in this last generation; and to share materials that will help prepare Christians for the troubled times to come.

Throughout Bible history and the largest portion of church history, God's people walked before the Lord with a holy fear. The lives of the ancient prophets, of the apostles, and of spiritual leaders in the modern era reveal a profound respect for His holiness and a great reverence for His awesome power. But this character quality of holy fear has been lost in our society. It has eroded particularly fast during the present generation.

The loss of holy fear within the Christian community means that end-time warnings lose much of their impact. It's relatively easy to mentally accept end-time chronology, to acknowledge that Christians are experiencing the happenings foretold in the Bible. But in order to make this message a life-changing revelation, it's necessary to accept it with a ready spirit. Accepting a teaching in one's spirit, rather than solely with the mind, requires a heart afraid to do *anything but* the will of God. *Holy Fear* invites Christians to develop the holy fear that is prerequisite to living the committed Christian life in these last days.

In the first chapter, I offer a brief description of our troubled times and point to the importance of holy fear. I then offer our own testimony. It's an account of how God led my wife Barbara and me to walk in fear of Him following a revelation my brother received in 1971. In the chapters that follow, I discuss Satan's method of attack during the end times, the spiritual harm it has done to American Christianity, and impending discipline through judgment. Judgment must come before spiritual commitment comes.

Much of the message in this book cannot be read casually. Facing spiritual attack, understanding the depth of moral deterioration, and preparing for judgment are not done for entertainment. Reading about these things should be unsettling. It should be distressing to come to terms with end-time happenings. It's also necessary to deal with them, because knowing what to expect in the troubled hours to come is the key to survival. It's like training soldiers for battle. Boot camp is not supposed to be fun. It's designed to harden new recruits and prepare them for the horror of the battlefield. Those who overcome their apathy and fear during the training stand a better chance of surviving when the real test comes.

Bob Fraley

Chapter 1

COURAGE THROUGH FEAR

How should Christians react to the last days in America? Jesus prophesied that the end of the Gentile Age would be dark and difficult. He compared the end times to the days of Noah:

> As it was in the days of Noah, so it will be at the coming of the Son of Man. For in the days before the flood, people were eating and drinking, marrying and giving in marriage, up to the day Noah entered the ark. (Matthew 24:37-38)

Many aspects of the end times mentioned in this verse are evident already. Consider divorce, for example. The phrase "marrying and giving in marriage" means that sincere commitment to marriage vows was lost and the people of Noah's day felt free to marry again and again. The same is true in our society today. The American divorce rate is more than 50 percent, nearly double that of any other country. Most divorced individuals remarry resulting in what sociologists call "serial monogamy." An extremely high divorce rate, however, is only one of many areas of moral deterioration in America. Americans, many Christians included, are wrapped-up in self-seeking pursuits and careless living. This has led to an even greater danger—an overall lack of respect for the standards of God. This was a major aspect of spiritual deterio-

ration in Noah's day, and it brought judgment in the form
of a worldwide flood.

THE TROUBLE WITH AMERICA

There are a lot of good things about this great nation.
God has blessed our land and it produces an agricultural
abundance. Our political ideals and legal traditions have
inspired many other peoples. Americans still enjoy one of
the highest standards of living in the world. But when it
comes to morality, America is not so great. Any Christian
willing to face reality must admit that we are in serious
trouble. The moral fiber that bound our nation and our
people together for centuries has unraveled. Our social
institutions have deteriorated to the point that what was
unthinkable a generation ago is now commonplace.

Even a glance at today's headlines reveals inexpress-
ible evil. Look at what is happening all around us:

- **The family, the most fundamental means of pre-
  serving social order, has been shattered.** Over the
  past three decades, the number of divorces affecting
  children has tripled to a million a year. As of 1988,
  ten million children lived with separated or divorced
  parents. Half of all children will experience the
  breakup of their parents' marriage, and 1 in 10 will
  suffer *three such marital dissolutions.* There were
  more than 450,000 runaways in 1988—children who
  left or stayed away from home for a night—although
  127,100 of these are more accurately termed "thrownaways." Thrownaways are children whose parents
  do not want them back, or who have abandoned
  them.[1]

- **Greed and unethical conduct have tainted profes-
  sions that have historically represented the "pil-
  lars of society."** Doctors, bankers, and other profes-

sionals have abandoned professional ethics in alarming numbers. In 1985 alone, as many as 4 million unnecessary surgical operations were performed. More than $10 billion is spent each year on unwarranted surgical procedures. Cases of financial institution fraud have skyrocketed. The number of failed financial institutions under FBI investigation jumped from 202 in 1986 to 670 in 1991. The number of convictions in major fraud cases (those cases in which reported losses exceed $100,000) shot up from 533 in 1986 to 1,043 in 1990.[2]

- **America's great cities, once the principle evidence of a mighty, industrial nation, are stalked by crime and violence.** Americans robbed, raped, assaulted, and murdered one another in record numbers in 1990. Robberies and aggravated assaults jumped 11 percent, forcible rape and murder shot up 9 percent. The nation's homicide toll reached an all-time high of 23,438 murders. Washington D.C., which should represent the seat of government, has become the crime capital of the world. This staggering increase in violent crime was matched only by the dramatic increase in correctional populations. As of 1987, an estimated 3.4 million adults were under some form of correctional supervision. From 1983 to 1987, parolees and probationers increased by 47 percent, prisoners and jail inmates increased by 33 percent. Today, 1 in 53 U.S. residents age 18 and older *is already under* some form of correctional supervision.[3]

- **Sexual immorality and life styles devoted to self-gratification have transformed the American character.** Sexually-transmitted diseases and substance abuse have reached epidemic proportions in many parts of the country. In Arizona, the incidence of syphilis increased to 26 per 100,000 residents in 1990, triple the 1988 rate. State health officials attributed the outbreak to increased sexual promiscuity and crack cocaine use. A 1991 report by a state board in South Carolina predicted that 15 percent of the state's adults would have serious problems with alcohol and drugs. More than 50,000 South Carolina residents entered drug addiction programs in 1990.[4]

- **Public schools, once the showpiece of a young democracy, have surrendered to drug abuse, sex, and criminal violence.** In 1988, 85 percent of high school seniors nationwide reported that they could obtain marijuana "fairly easy" or "very easily." That figure was 63.9 percent for amphetamines, 50.3 percent for cocaine powder, and 28.0 percent for heroin. In Texas, a 1991 Commission on Alcohol and Drug Abuse survey designed to measure the age of first-time drug abusers found that 57 percent of the state's sixth-graders and 39 percent of fifth-graders have tried alcohol. Sexual activity within our schools is higher than ever before. According to a 1991 survey by the Atlanta-based Center for Disease Control, more than half of the nation's high schoolers have had sex. Over 70 percent of students have had sex by their twelfth year. Crime competes with drugs and sex as the most serious problem facing public education. In Chicago, a 200-member police force assigned to patrol the public schools made 2,000 arrests during the first eight months after the unit was formed in September, 1990. Included in the total were 169 arrests for robbery, 187 for aggravated battery, and 189 for aggravated assault. In addition, police confiscated 147 guns at the schools and 339 other weapons.[5]

- **Our government has turned its back on the scriptural principles that formed the moral foundation of this nation.** Our government has outlawed the expression of Christianity in public life. Banning school prayer was only the beginning. In 1989, the U.S. Supreme Court declared a nativity scene on the lawn of a Pittsburgh courthouse unconstitutional. Yet Christians are prohibited from nonviolent protests of abortion clinics. In June 1991, the Los Angeles Police Department finally agreed to an out-of-court settlement to stop using martial arts weapons called nunchakus against Operation Rescue volunteers who nonviolently protest abortion.[6]

- **Americans have reserved their most vicious attack for children, who once embodied the best the American people had to offer.** One and a half million abortions are performed each year. Abortion has become an acceptable form of birth control. Of those children that survive the womb, millions more are abused and neglected. In 1987, more than 2.1 million children were reported to have been abused, neglected, or both. The rate of child abuse and neglect reports has increased steadily every year reliable statistics are available. In 1982, the rate was 20.1 per 100,000; by 1987 the rate had climbed to 34.0. Countless others are emotionally and mentally impaired. During the past thirty years both the homicide and suicide rates for children have increased threefold.[7]

Yet as disturbing as these statistics are, they do not tell the whole story. Cold, hard facts cannot convey the tragedy of a Houston woman who delivered her baby two-months premature in the bathroom of a crack house. The woman received a twelve-year sentence for cocaine possession when an autopsy revealed a fatal dose of the drug in the baby's liver. Statistics do not account for the calamity of a drive-by execution of a deaf woman walking along a Los Angeles street last summer. Apparently, the shooting was triggered by a sign-language conversation with her companion that was mistaken for a rival gang's hand-signal. Nor can the facts and figures describe the awfulness of a Dallas man who sold his four-year-old son to crack dealers. Not sure with what to charge the man, police considered assault and child-selling charges against the man who sold the boy for $40.[8]

AS IT WAS IN THE DAYS OF NOAH...

Satan has released all the hordes of hell in this last generation culminating in unheard of cultural upheavals. It is only a slight exaggeration to say that 1990s America has discarded the biblical standards on which our nation was founded as fast as yesterday's news. Satan has undermined our families, our public schools, our government, our way of thinking, and our social order. We are engaged in no less than a spiritual war for America's heritage.

We live in a society devoted to pleasure and self-gratification. "If you can get away with it, then it is alright" is the slogan of many Americans today. Personal accountability, respect for authority, and self-control have become antiquated thinking from bygone days. Americans consume a steady diet of conventional wisdom that says aggressive behavior is O.K.; any sort of sexuality is fine so long as it's fun; if you really love liberty you will ridicule and poke fun at God-fearing Christians; and that abusive language and profanity is an acceptable way to express yourself. Movies, TV programs, music, magazines, and books preach a message of cultural relativism: nothing is indecent or repugnant, rules are prohibited, everything is permissible, nothing deserves to be honored and respected.

People's ability to draw the line between right and wrong, good and bad, beautiful and ugly, meaningful and ritualistic, has been erased. The Enemy has been frighteningly successful in reaching his objective in the spiritual warfare in which we are now engaged. Seeking the character quality of holy fear has been lost and forgotten. Finding someone with a strong conscience against sin is rare.

The new wave of "Me First!" thinking helps explain how our culture has sanctioned the murder of over 25 million babies as an exercise in personal freedom. It was in 1973 that the country's highest court declared abortion legal. Since then, we have witnessed a ghastly sacrifice of human life to the god of self. Abortion should be an eye-opening illustration of the self-serving spirit that has swept across our land in this last generation. We may not be guilty of abortion personally, but we need to constantly be on guard that the spirit behind such a dreadful act does not also sweep us into its grip and reveal itself through some other self-serving activity.

Recently, Chuck Colson stated in his message on the "Secularization of America," that the people in America have lost their courage to stand up for true values. I believe he is right. Once we lose our courage to stand up for what we know is right, we will lose everything worth fighting for. The tally on the scoreboard of life, which reflects the values being taught and followed by many, reveals that not only is this statement true, but that it is happening at a very accelerated pace.

There is a constant flow of books, newsletters, pamphlets, tracts, and magazine articles from Christian organizations that document the moral decline of America. Many well-informed Christian leaders have addressed this issue at this critical hour of our spiritual history. The rotten fruit produced by our society is there for all to see, and Jesus said that we can know the health of a plant by looking at its fruit. There is no excuse for any Christian to be uninformed.

I know it is depressing to have to think about the fact that Satan's forces have besieged our country. There are those who will disagree and claim that Christians are not losing the spiritual battle for our land. Our emotions, our flesh, would prefer to ignore such bad news. It's difficult to accept such rottenness, but we cannot afford to put our heads in the sand. Things will only get worse. How will we survive these last hours if we are not prepared for them?

WHAT IS HOLY FEAR?

And now I return to the question with which this chapter began: How should Christians react to the last days in America? Rest assured that as dark as it gets, there is hope for God's people. In reference to Noah living in the worldly conditions of his day, the Bible tells us:

> By faith Noah, when warned about things not yet seen, in *holy fear* built an ark to save his family. (Hebrews 11:7)

This verse speaks of Noah's faith, of his being warned of things to come, and about how his "holy fear" led him to take action to save his family. Since our times are similar to Noah's, it stands to reason that Christians need to have the same attitude of heart Noah had in order to face the pressures, temptations, and trials. Christians should react to the "days of Noah" the same way that Noah did.

It was Noah's fear of the Lord that saved him. His holy fear saved him and his family from God's judgment in his day (the flood), and that same attitude of heart can preserve us through the tribulations in our own time. Although Scripture speaks of the importance of holy fear, I do not find a precise definition. Deuteronomy 31:12

reads "Learn to fear the Lord your God." Psalm 33:8 pro-
claims, "Let all the earth fear the Lord," and Psalm 34:7
says "The angel of the Lord encamps around those who
fear him." 1 Peter 1:17 contains the commandment: "live
your lives as strangers here in reverent fear," and Acts
9:31 reports that the early church "grew in numbers, living in the fear of the Lord."

To me, holy fear means to stand in awe of, and have a
deep respect for, God's holiness and His standards. Christians with this characteristic possess an inner desire to
avoid sin in every aspect of their lives. There is a conscious desire to steer clear of anything that would dis-
please the Lord. Obedience becomes the utmost priority.
Proverbs 16:6 says: "Through the fear of the Lord a man
avoids evil." Proverbs 8:13 instructs: "To fear the Lord is
to hate evil." To live in holy fear means to seek God's will
in all things, and to examine every aspect of life according to the Word of God. Fear of being outside God's will
becomes the driving force behind every thought and
every action. Holy fear develops the desire to subject
everything in our lives to the same exacting standard: "Is
this pleasing to Him?" Holy fear gives us discernment.

It's not that the sinful nature is inactive. It rises up in
our minds and battles for control over our decisions
about how to act. I am not saying that a Christian will
have total victory over sin. Only Jesus lived a life of moral
perfection. In my own life, I know that if I allow the old
nature to grab control of my thoughts, I lose compassion
for others and develop an argumentative spirit. But as I
allow the Lord to open my spiritual eyes, I see the ways of
my heart, and I become convicted and repentant.

As Christians, keeping ourselves in line requires the
proper amount of fear. Our heart's desire should be to
walk in a manner pleasing to Him. But as we walk in the
comfort of the Holy Spirit and His blessing, which is a
spiritual concept, it is easy to begin taking some things

for granted. It's easy to lose that fear of God's expectations that we need to remain healthy spiritually. Jesus
always kept his eyes on the mark. He avoided sin at every
turn. He never wavered. If we live before the Lord with a
holy fear, we will be doing the thing that will enable us to
stay true to Him. We will not deviate so easily from God's
standards or be led astray by worldly standards or those
who have gotten off the track. Worldly ideas and activities are very attractive for Christians today, but Jesus
avoided them because He saw things in the light of
eternity. As in the song by Keith Green:

> O Lord, you're beautiful,
> Your face is all I seek;
> for when your eyes are on this child
> your grace abounds to me.
> O Lord, please light the fire
> that once burned bright and clear;
> replace the lamp of my first love,
> that burns with *holy fear!*[9]

One area where holy fear is desperately needed today
is parent-child relationships. Parents who desire a Christian life style for their children face major confrontations
due to the tremendous worldly pressure pushing our
youth in the opposite direction. Many of these parents
have given up the fight for their families. "I've had
enough! I can't take the hassle anymore," they confess, "I
just don't have the energy to keep up the struggle." They
feel bad because they must correct their children and say
"no" so often, and they become willing to compromise
because it's easier. God's anointing of holy fear is what
exasperated parents need. It takes something stronger
than personal willpower to find the strength to carry on,
to stand firm, and to fight constant family battles. Winning over Satan as parents begins with the fear of the

Lord; He will keep those who seek Him from giving in and giving up. Proverbs 22:6 shows that this is so important.

There is no easy way to develop a fearful attitude toward God. There is no set of tapes you can buy, no church activity you can do, no step-by-step program you can follow. It is not a matter of personal willpower, nor of accomplishing a certain goal. Really, it is not something you do at all; it is something God does to you when you are honest with Him. But if your standards as a Christian allow you to walk along the edge of darkness, then it is a sure indication that you do not have the kind of relationship with God I am talking about. Christians should strive to stay as far away as possible from worldly standards and give no advantage to Satan. Our habit of mind should be the strong desire to avoid sin at every turn, to walk uprightly in a manner pleasing to Him, and to live in awe of the Lord.

Noah received a revelation about God's plan for judging the world. The warning revealed to him developed the quality of holy fear within his character, and this character trait motivated him to adhere to God's standards. In his day, Godly standards had been lost. But the depth of his reliance on God and his love of God's ways led him to walk by faith, build an ark, and save his family. In my own life, there has been a similar sequence of events. After a revelation from the Lord about the end times, Barbara and I began to walk in holy fear, and through the Lord's faithfulness we have been able to raise our family in these desperate times. All nine of our children love and serve the Lord.

COURAGE THROUGH FEAR

In his October 15, 1990 newsletter, David Wilkerson wrote: "the Apostle Paul warns us that 'in the last days perilous times shall come'" (2 Timothy 3:1 KJV). Paul's use of the word "perilous" means dangerous, fierce, and violent times that sap Christians' strength. Those times are here. It's the days of Noah all over again. Things are only going to get worse. Judgment awaits around the corner. So we must do what Noah did. We start with fear of the Lord. Those who fear the Lord have nothing to be afraid of from the world in the days to come no matter what happens. That is because in God's kingdom, *great courage against the Enemy begins with fear of the Lord.*

Chapter 2

OUR TESTIMONY

During the past twenty years, my wife Barbara and I have done a number of things that have appeared to be quite incomprehensible to our relatives and friends. To many of those who have known us along the way, we made a series of puzzling, seemingly irrational decisions. We added six children to our family when we were in our early thirties and had two boys of our own. I gave up a position as vice president of a thriving company without having another job. We left a beautiful new home we had built to suit our needs for an uncertain future across the country. Some of the things we have experienced seem incredulous to Barbara and me. We were put on trial by a church we both loved. We helped found a Christian school when neither of us planned on a career in education. I have become a "Christian author" when I dislike writing so much I will seldom write a letter.

The best way for me to explain why we did what we did is to say that we possessed a holy fear of the Lord. Following a tragic accident and a visit with my brother, Barbara and I developed an earnest desire to follow the Lord's direction regardless of the consequences. Then God led me to found Christian Life Services in order to share several messages with the church, which in turn led me to write this book. Maybe I should begin at the beginning.

Early Years

I was raised on a hundred-acre farm in southwestern Ohio. Both my parents were deeply committed to the Lord Jesus Christ. People who knew my mother testify that she lived an exemplary Christian life much like the outstanding Godly women of the Bible. I made my first commitment to the Lord Jesus when I was nine years old. I still remember being baptized in a muddy creek that cut through our farm.

When my high school days ended and I left home for college, the spiritual truth in 1 Corinthians 15:33 (KJV), "Do not be deceived: bad company ruins good morals," became a reality in my life. Although I was an upstanding citizen by secular standards, I wandered in the world for the next twelve years. After marrying Barbara, a Christian girl from my hometown, I influenced her to accept some of my worldly ways.

I was 29 when the spiritual foundation I had received in my youth began to minister to my heart. I know that my mother's devotion to praying for me was one of the reasons I experienced an inner drive to read the Bible with an open heart. Within a few months, Barbara and I recommitted our lives to the Lord Jesus. Serving the Lord became the center of our activities.

Barbara was known as "Mrs. Energy" because she could get so much accomplished in a day. Her boundless gift of hospitality was put to full use by the Lord. It would be difficult to count the number of times over the past 25 years, we have had from 25 to 150 people to our home for a sit-down dinner, served hot and fresh complete with decorations. The Spirit of the Lord ministered comfort and peace in a heart-warming atmosphere of love and tranquility. Many times, visitors commented that they just did not want to leave. Many say that Barbara is one of the wittiest individuals they have ever met. Her gift to cheer the heart as good medicine (Proverbs 17:22) has been a blessing and a joy to many.

The first few years of our recommitment passed quickly. We kept ourselves busy raising our two sons, serving in our church, and helping neighbors and friends. I became vice president and general manager of Benada Aluminum Company, a growing Youngstown, Ohio, firm that manufactured aluminum extrusions. Barbara and I purchased 15 acres near Poland, Ohio, and we began thinking about building a home. Everything was coming together.

A TRAGEDY UNITES TWO FAMILIES

Then on Saturday, October 4, 1969, everything changed. Barbara and I had gone to Detroit to visit friends and it was late in the evening when we returned home to Youngstown, Ohio. We had left Perry, our oldest son, with our minister for the day, and stopped there to pick him up. It was then we learned of the tragedy that had happened earlier in the day. One of the elders from our church, along with his wife and three of their six children had been in an automobile accident. They had been driving in the country that afternoon when a pick-up truck missed a stop sign and hit the front half of their station wagon broadside at full speed. Both parents were killed instantly.

I left for the hospital immediately. When I arrived, I discovered that Andrea, their ten-year-old daughter, had a fractured skull and such severe brain damage that she was pronounced hopeless. Hospital staff had decided to leave the usual patient-cleanup procedure to the mortuary. Alice, four years old, was on the critical list. Sixteen-year-old Larry had escaped with only minor cuts and bruises.

Six More Children

As I drove home from the hospital in the early hours of that Sunday morning, I experienced something new in my relationship with the Lord. For the first time, He spoke directly to me through His indwelling Holy Spirit. I heard no audible voice, but what I heard was clearly and unmistakably divine. He said: "Build a new house on the land you recently bought and take these six orphaned children to raise."

I later discovered the Lord had revealed this same message to Barbara. At first, the additional responsibility seemed too much to handle. We were already busy at home, work, and church, and now the Lord wanted us to care for six more children. Four of them were teenagers! But we prayed, and He made it clear that He would supply the patience, the power, and the wisdom. It is important for you to understand that we did not take these children to raise because we were sympathetic, tender-hearted humanitarians bent on saving the world. Nor was it because we were "superspiritual Christians," nor because it was "our thing" to raise a big family. Barbara and I were not seeking anything additional to do because at the time of the accident, our lives were rich and full. Our relatives and friends said, "You don't need such an added responsibility in your lives. Everything is so perfect in your home. You have so much going for you." But the Lord did not reveal to them what He revealed to us.

Jesus promises to provide us with what we need to carry out his appointments. In John 15:16, Jesus says: "You did not choose me, but I chose you and appointed you to go and bear fruit—fruit that will last. Then the Father will give you whatever you ask in my name." He chose us for this task, and over the years He has continued to work out every detail.

Legally, the children coming to live with us was complicated by the fact that the children's parents had not left a will, and we had never met any of their extended family. The children's relatives immediately objected to our parenting them. But after several meetings—and no one knows why except that it was the hand of the Lord—the state probate judge appointed us legal guardians and our new family became a reality. Marilyn, the oldest, was eighteen. She roomed with Brenda fifteen, Mary thirteen, Andrea ten, and Alice, age four. Larry, at seventeen, moved in with our sons Perry, age eleven, and Greg, who was three. Our youngest son, Michael, was born in 1976.

A Bonus for Andrea

Solving legal problems was only the beginning of the Lord's intervention. Unexpectedly, Andrea lived through the first night, and so she was transferred to a hospital closer to home. We were told that surgery was necessary, although the attending physician warned us that even if the procedure was successful Andrea could not return to school until the following fall— eleven months away. Even then, she would never make a complete recovery but would be disabled, both physically and mentally, for life.

But the Lord completely reversed the brain damage she received. She returned to school within three weeks of the accident. The surgeons never operated. When the Lord healed Andrea, He gave her a bonus. From the time she was a baby, she had had a malfunctioning kidney. She took medicine twice a day, and had been under a doctor's care since birth. She was often sick, and at ten years of age weighed only 41 pounds. The Lord healed this abnormal kidney. Kidney medicine and frequent visits to the doctor became a thing of the past. Her weight doubled to

82 pounds within a year, and she changed from that of a frail, sickly child to a strong, robust child. Today, Andrea, her husband, and their four boys operate a 500-head dairy farm near Phoenix, Arizona.

Part Two of the Lord's Command

Barbara and I had obeyed part one of the Lord's command, "Take these children to raise," but there was also part two: "Build a new house on the land you recently bought." Barbara and I, now the parents of eight children, became acutely aware of the need for a bigger house. We had already purchased land and had planned to build. So we chose a set of house plans, found a general contractor, and signed a contract.

We knew that in order for things to work out financially we would need to sell our old house quickly. Once again, we praised God for His faithfulness. He brought us a buyer before we could list the house with a realtor, and not only that, the buyer paid us our asking price in advance though he knew he would not get possession for six months, the time required to build our new house. We were amazed and grateful for what the Lord did when we were obedient to His commands. We had to get the equity out of our old house immediately in order to have the cash to build a new one.

By the time the ten of us settled into our new home, it was evident that the Lord had used the construction of this new house to mold us into a family. There was a lot of work involved, and we all took part in making our new house a home. We decorated the bedrooms, living room, and other interior areas, then cleared about five acres. We leveled and seeded a two-acre lawn, and cultivated another acre for a garden. As the brush piles grew and then shrank, our two families had become one.

Soon, our new home became a hub for church gatherings. We often invited the entire congregation over for picnics, games, and fellowship. There was a large lawn for potlucks and volleyball, a stream to wade in, and a woods for firewood and children's games. We enjoyed our new home, and many visitors did too.

THE REVELATION

In June 1971, about a year and a half after taking the children, another word came from the Lord. This time, the Lord made the principles in Hebrews 11:7 an inner working truth in my life. "By faith Noah," the verse begins, "when warned about things not yet seen, in holy fear built an ark to save his family."

We hosted a giant picnic at our place that Memorial Day, and two weekends later took a trip to southwestern Ohio. We visited Barbara's parents, spent some time with my mother, and then on Sunday, stopped to see Charles, my brother two years older than I. (There were thirteen children in our family; I am the youngest.) Charles, who is now a missionary surgeon in Kenya, Africa, told me of the revelation he had had concerning the identity of the end-time beast of Revelation 13:3. (The details of this revelation appear in Chapter 3.)

At the moment Charles shared the revelation with me, I experienced something that never happened before. An overwhelming anointing from the Lord fell on me. I trembled before the Lord as His presence became so real. I had to know whether what Charles had said agreed with the Word of God. As I studied prophetic scriptures, commentaries, and other books for confirmation of Charles's revelation, I discovered that there are many different views on the exact meaning of the symbolic words which describe the characteristics of the beast. I could not gain any peaceful understanding from the Lord and so I concluded: "When and if the Lord wants me to know the exact meaning of other prophetic Scriptures, He will show me." I had no idea that finding the answers would mean writing a book and being separated from our church fellowship—the Enemy struck where it would hurt the most.

Write a Book

But one night, about a year after our visit with Charles, I received another divine message. As I was praying, the Lord spoke again in my inner man as He had following the accident that brought six children into our family. He said: "Write a book for your brother about the identity of the beast."

I had no idea how to write a book or even where to begin. Even worse, I disliked writing. This may sound unbelievable to you because you know me as an author but within my heart I know I would not write anything if I did not have to. I experience such heaviness when I begin to put my thoughts on paper that only the Lord's strength prevents me from stopping before I get started. In fact, when I attended Miami University at Oxford, Ohio, to study mathematics, I failed my first attempt at English composition. I repeated the course only because it was required to graduate. But now, knowing I had heard the voice of the Lord, my only thought was to follow His command. I decided to trust in His grace and power, and I committed myself to the task.

Resigning My Job

Not knowing what was involved, I figured I could write the book in a few weeks. As I began to collect my sources and put my thoughts on paper, I soon discovered that writing is a process, not an act. About that time, I sensed an inner burden that I was to resign from my job. As a company vice-president, my work was enjoyable and very rewarding, but I had perfect peace about this decision. I trusted the Lord would provide another position when the book was finished.

I remember well the day I planned to tender my resignation. It was such a busy day that I completely forgot about it. I did not realize something was wrong until I got in my car to go home that evening. As I pulled out of the parking lot, I felt such a strong force within that I will never forget it. Something was awry spiritually, but I did not know what. I quickly reviewed the day's events in search of an answer, but came up empty. The pressure mounted. It became so strong that I stopped along the road about half way home. I began to pray, and to ask the Lord for forgiveness (for what I did not know), and then the cause of my problem became clear: *I had been so devoted to my job that I had forgotten to quit!* I was heartbroken. I had broken my promise with the Lord.

I immediately confessed and He lifted my heavy feeling. Peace and joy returned to my spirit. First thing next morning, I turned in my letter of resignation. I had been scheduled to fly to New York, but the trip was postponed until a later date. A few days later I went to work fulltime as a writer.

The first six weeks went smoothly. I studied prophetic Scriptures in Daniel, 2 Thessalonians, 1 John, and Revelation. The cryptic sentences and symbolic imagery began to make sense, not because I had figured it out, but because the Lord revealed the hidden meaning. I realize that such a statement will raise a few eyebrows, but I can testify that the Lord's revelations on these prophetic Scriptures were true. I had heard the word of the Lord before, and I recognized His voice.

REVELATION ON TRIAL

A few months after my work on the book began, Barbara and I experienced a vicious attack from the Enemy. The attack came through some of our dearest Christian friends; people with whom we had worshipped, served, and fellowshipped for years. We spent time with them four to five times a week and they became our accusers.

As I wrote about the revelation Charles received, the Lord guided me to study two books by the great Chinese Christian, Watchman Nee. I read *Love Not The World* and *The Normal Christian Life.* The spiritual principles contained in Nee's *The Normal Christian Life* seemed so important given what I had come to know about spiritual warfare and walking in the power of God's spirit that I read the book three times, outlined it from cover to cover, and shared it with my adult Sunday School class. That's when the trouble started.

Just after the morning worship one Sunday, I heard that a "secret" deacons meeting was underway. I wondered why no one had told me about it earlier especially since I was a deacon. As I walked into the meeting room, there was complete silence. Then, several fellow deacons and our minister—one of my closest friends—criticized my teaching. They questioned what I had told my class regarding the amount of faith Christians should possess. Next came a volley of allegations. They accused me of things I had not done, and they questioned my motivation for teaching. I was shocked, and saddened.

What followed hurt even more. The men of the church conducted an ecclesiastical trial, leveled another round of unfounded accusations, then banished Barbara and me from fellowship. No one explained the rationale for this drastic action except to say that I had falsely taught how much faith Christians could place in the indwelling Holy Spirit to guide their lives. At first I planned to boycott the trial, but the night before, while I was praying, I knew the Lord wanted me to attend. At first it was very rough, but later I had a chance to speak. I shared the Spirit's fruit of love and kindness with those attending for nearly three hours. This was not an expression of my nature, but a witness of God's nature. Hardly anyone spoke on our behalf during the meeting, but later several of those present told me they had witnessed God's anointing as I spoke that night.

After the trial, Barbara and I were no longer accepted by most of the congregation. Our home, once the center of church activities, was pronounced off limits. Barbara and I felt rejected. People we admired and respected scorned us, close friends abandoned us. As the days passed we realized that what had taken place was not the fault of these dear friends at all, but rather was the work of Satan. We were "battling not against flesh and blood..." (Ephesians 6:10).

In the days that followed, the loss of fellowship took its toll. Work on the book manuscript came to a standstill. For a while, it certainly appeared as if Satan was going to win. Deep depression sapped our energy. The deep-seated awareness that Jesus was in our hearts guiding our way was gone. He seemed indifferent and remote.

Victory

I remember the day the clouds lifted as if it were yesterday. A close sister in the Lord called and said: "We just have to continuously keep our eyes on Jesus and take them off ourselves in situations such as you're in." I knew this truth well, but had not applied it to my own situation. As she spoke, the Holy Spirit ministered to me. It was like something snapped within my inner being and I was released from the Enemy's deadly grip. Soon I was back at work on the book. I finished the first draft in a few weeks and a good friend typed it for me—all 650 pages.

I thought my days of writing were nearly over but found out they had only just begun. This first manuscript required a great deal of editing, and I soon learned that editing takes longer than writing. But before this task began, the Lord dealt with another area in our family that we had been praying about and seeking His guidance on for some time.

MAKING THE RIGHT MOVE

As Barbara and I became increasingly aware of the beast-system and its influence, we realized the importance of providing a proper spiritual education for our children. We taught our children about God at home but we were also concerned about what they were learning away from home. The Lord showed us that by sending our children to the public school, we were saddling them with a heavy weight. At their tender age, we were asking them to cope with the humanistic indoctrination and worldly pressures within the public school system.

The Importance of Christian Education

This leading was consistent with the Word of God. Many Scriptures outline parental duties. As stewards of God's children, we are to teach (Deuteronomy 6:7), to train (Proverbs 22:6), to provide for (2 Corinthians 12:14; 1 Timothy 5:8), to nurture (Ephesians 6:4), to control (1 Timothy 3:4, 12), and to love (Titus 2:4). According to Scripture, it is of the utmost importance for Christian children to be educated by born-again believers in a wholesome, uplifting atmosphere. School days should be filled with pleasant memories and character-building experiences based on the Word of God. The primary verse the Lord gave us about the importance of Christian education was Psalm 1:1-2 which says, "Blessed is the man who *does not walk in the counsel of* [or take instruction from] the wicked or stand in the way of sinners or sit in the seat of mockers. But his delight is in the law of the Lord, and on his law he meditates day and night."

We needed a Christian school for our children, but there were none in our community at that time. So we scouted several parts of the country to find the place God wanted us. We visited Christian schools in Georgia, Florida, and Alabama, but we could not find peace about a move to any of these locations. Then, while journeying back to Ohio, the Lord pointed us to Phoenix, Arizona.

Barbara and I traveled to Phoenix just after New Year's. By the end of our week's visit things started to fall into place. We found Christian elementary and secondary schools. We made an offer on a house, but since neither Barbara nor I were employed, the bankers needed some time to think. And although our offer had not been accepted when we flew back to Ohio, we prepared to leave as soon as we returned. We trusted that God would have everything ready by the time we moved West.

But leaving the new home we had made for ourselves was difficult. I still marvel at Barbara's spiritual outlook in that situation. She had designed the interior, selected the decorations, and coordinated the furnishings. Everything was perfect, yet she was willing to follow God's direction regardless. Worldly wisdom would have convinced us to stay, that a move to find different schools was not worth it, but our walk before the Lord in holy fear meant to walk in obedience, so we were determined to follow the Holy Spirit's leading.

So much had to be done in such a short period of time. We packed all our household and personal items and completed the sale of our Ohio house. Final papers were approved the last possible day. We sold our lawn and garden equipment (there is not as much grass to mow in Phoenix), and auctioned off what items would not fit in two U-Haul trucks. We cleaned our house one last time, then said goodbye to our friends.

A day later, our convoy began the 2,250 mile trek to the Valley of the Sun. I drove one of the rented trucks pulling our pickup. Larry, our oldest guardian son, drove the other with our station wagon in tow, and Barbara drove our car with a travel trailer behind.

What Almost Happened in New Mexico

All along the way we witnessed evidence that God was watching over us. One particular sign of His faithfulness occurred during our fifth night on the road.

We had planned to spend the night in a trailer park in a small town in New Mexico. I arrived two hours ahead of Barbara and Larry, so I checked in, found a spot for the trailer, and secured a parking place for the trucks. As Perry, Greg—our two oldest sons—and I passed the time, a carload of men drove by. They stopped for a few seconds, then drove away. A deep sense of foreboding came over me and I felt that it was not safe to stay where we were. I shook off the feeling, but it returned a few minutes later. I tried to put it out of my mind.

As the minutes ticked by, my fearful feeling intensified. By the time Barbara and Larry caught up with us, I had left the trailer park and was waiting along side the highway. Danger awaited if we stayed although what kind of danger I could not say. Although the next trailer park was four hours away, the fuel tanks were empty, and everyone was travel-weary, we pressed on. It was 2:30 in the morning before we found the next KOA in Benson, Arizona.

Everyone awoke early the last day of our trip. The kids were anxious to get their first look at Arizona. When we arrived in Phoenix our house was ready as we trusted it would be, and soon the trucks were unloaded. Mary, Perry, Andrea, Alice, and Greg started school and Barbara set to work making our new house comfortable and familiar. I returned to my task as author and eventually retyped 650 pages. As I reflected on the preceding series of events and my present situation, I had to smile. Eight months ago I was a business executive with a personal secretary, now I was jobless and doing my own typing. God was so good!

Only then did we discover why we left New Mexico in such a hurry that night. I ran into several people familiar with New Mexico and they repeated the same amazing story. It seems a ring of thieves plagued the town where we planned to spend the night. Trucks parked overnight were the prime target. The ring's *modus operandi* was to pull up next to the victim's truck with a bigger truck, clean it out, then head for the mountains. Do-it-yourself moving vans were the thieves' choice because they were filled with fast-selling household items and were driven by displaced persons. One man I met told me that he had grown up in that crime-ridden town, and had no doubt that had we stayed we would have lost everything.

Another man confirmed this likelihood with a personal experience. His family had stopped to rest in that same park a few weeks earlier. Like us, they had rented a U-Haul. But they awoke the next morning to find they had been robbed. Everything they owned disappeared without a trace. Imagine how grateful we were to have had the Lord's protection.

Six months passed before I completed the second draft of the book. I had condensed the manuscript to 400 pages and was confident I had produced the finished product. But a professional writer I consulted said the manuscript still needed more work. This was discouraging, at first. Then the Holy Spirit refreshed me and I returned to my typewriter.

Starting a School

Since the reason we moved to Arizona was for the children's education, I had no idea that within a year after we arrived, the Christian grade school our children attended would fold. I had no idea that Barbara and I would help start another one either.

In January 1974, Golden West Christian School—the school our children attended—declared bankruptcy. An organization located in Hawthorne, California, which had operated the school, placed it into receivership. Parents were notified that the school would close in two weeks. But a group of parents called a meeting, and decided to make an attempt to keep the school going in order to finish out the four months left in the school year. I traveled to California to meet with the law firm handling the receivership, and we reached an agreement to allow the school to continue until the end of the year.

When the spring term ended, the Association of Christian Schools International contacted me about opening a Christian school in northeastern Phoenix. I was receptive to the idea, but I knew that starting a school would be difficult. We needed an administrator for one thing. We also needed facilities. No school could open without a building, textbooks, desks, chalkboards, playground equipment and so on. With only two and a half months to go before the start of the next school year, it seemed impossible. But Barbara and I sought the Lord, and with two other couples, made a commitment to begin a new Christian school.

After several days of prayer and fasting, we began to see the Lord at work. First, He brought us an administrator. In June, we hired Elroy Ratzlaff, a school administrator with twenty years experience. He and his wife Erma, had come to Phoenix two years earlier to work as missionaries on the Gila River Indian Reservation, and in June of that year, they believed the Lord was guiding them to return to Christian education. Now we had an administrator. We still needed a building—and everything else.

God continued to work. Just a few days after we found our new administrator, I received a call from a man in Washington, D.C., who told me he owned a parcel of land in northeast Phoenix. He said the property included a building that had been used for a school. The school had been closed for several years, but all instructional materials were intact. The classrooms were equipped with chalkboards, desks, and chairs; there were textbooks and teaching materials for grades kindergarten through eight; and there were playground facilities for small children, plus an acre and a half that could be converted into additional play areas. I did not know anything about this man, and he never said how he found my name. Needless to say, we inspected the property and found that it was ideal. We signed a two-year lease, refurbished the buildings and grounds, and hired a teaching staff.

Paradise Valley Christian School opened its doors in the fall of 1974 with 37 students. Through the years, enrollment has grown, teaching and administrative staffs have expanded, and we have moved to larger facilities. This has been a wonderful experience for Barbara and me. We have directed school operations over the years, and we have watched as it has become one of the major schools in Phoenix (kindergarten through eighth grade). Children attend from more than 50 churches representing many different denominations.

ANOTHER JOB FOR FATHER

In the meantime, a year went by since I had left my job in Ohio. I wrote and rewrote. We had no income during that time but had managed financially due to the sale of our Ohio property. Another three months passed, and I became aware of the fact that I needed to find another job. I awoke one morning to hear that clear, inner voice of the Spirit of the Lord. I was to search for a job. I could finish what was left of the book during evenings and weekends if I hired someone to type the corrected copy.

I investigated several career possibilities before I heard about a metallurgical engineer planning to start an aluminum company similar to the one I had helped manage in Ohio. My initial meeting with him was very favorable. He valued my many years of successful business experi-

ence but he was concerned that I would demand a sub-
stantial income to match. He knew that it would be difficult for his new company starting out, but I was confident
that I should sign on. So I told him I would accept whatever salary he could afford. If I received a thousand dollars a month, it would be okay; I would help him build his
company.

My heart overflowed with the joy of the Lord when he
called to offer me a management position. Barbara and I
praised God, and with tears in our eyes, we thanked Him
for his faithfulness. I had not worked for 15 months while
I was busy writing, and now, the Lord let me return to the
industry I knew best. His timing was perfect. I would not
have been looking for a job at that point had the Lord not
spoken to me that morning a few weeks before.

Since helping start Pimalco Incorporated 18 years ago,
the Lord has provided untold wisdom. This fledgling company that began on a shoestring in 1973 has become the
most successful operation of its kind in the world.
Pimalco's achievement in the aluminum business surprised industry analysts because the company has been
consistently able to profitably make a very complex
product during a time when most other companies
(including large companies like Reynolds Aluminum, Martin Marietta and Kaiser Aluminum) have closed similar
plants due to the difficulty of making the product and
their poor profit performance in general. Pimalco manu-
factures high-strength, high-tech, metallurgical aluminum
alloys for the aerospace industry. Our materials are used
by all the major aircraft builders including Boeing,
McDonnell-Douglas, General Dynamics, Grumman, North-
rup, Lockheed, Beech, Cessna and others for passenger,
transport, military and private aircraft alike. The company now employs more than 400 people with a payroll of
over $1 million per month. Our annual sales
volume runs between $80 to $90 million. We have three

plants located on 26 acres in an industrial park just outside of Phoenix.

To achieve such a position of industry leadership in quality, promise performance, customer service, and integrity has required a team effort. Many dedicated people work together to produce a sophisticated metallurgical product in a peaceful, congenial atmosphere. Even to outside observers, it really appears as if something extraordinary happened. Only God's wisdom and guidance could have directed our efforts to make us so successful while at the same time every other similar high-tech aluminum extrusion plant in the country is struggling or closed.

BECOMING AN AUTHOR

After another year of work on the manuscript, I received peace from the Lord that the book was finally near completion. *God Reveals the Identity of the Beast* rolled off the press in 1975 four and a half years after the visit I had with my brother on the farm in Ohio. The years went by and the Lord continued to teach me. As I learned more about the end-times happenings God had warned about, I rewrote that first book and updated the message. It was republished in 1984 under a new title, *The Last Days in America.*

Over 100,000 copies of this message have now been sold. If I correctly understand the criteria for Christian book sales, it qualifies as a national best-seller. Even more interesting to me than the amount of sales per se is that most of these books were sold without advertising. No marketing campaign, no publicity tour occurred. Only a handful of Christian bookstores in the country are aware of the book, so most have not stocked it. This book has simply been sold from book racks in grocery stores and through the mail by Christian Life Services, an organization founded for the purpose of distributing the book and other Christian literature.

After publishing *The Last Days in America,* the Lord burdened me with additional messages for His people. These messages concerned Satan's methods of spiritual warfare and his many-sided attack on traditional biblical Christian standards in our country. To share these messages, I was inspired by the Lord to periodically write a newsletter.

My first newsletter was published in 1986. To help prepare the way, God sent Gideon Miller, a dedicated servant of the Lord and a long time friend and minister of the Word of God, from Salzburg, Austria. Gideon visited Barbara and me during the winter of 1985-86. His spirit sensed that he was to begin an extended fast to help endure a spiritual battle concerning what the Lord was going to begin working through me. He fasted for thirty days. I joined him the last two weeks, eating a meal every third day since I continued to work in my job. It was out of that time of fasting and seeking the Lord that I received the Lord's guidance to write a newsletter.

I entitled that first newsletter, "The Last Days in America," the same title as the book. Today there are approximately 95,000 people around the country on the Christian Life Services mailing list who receive my newsletters. There has been a particular vision or revelation from the Lord behind each newsletter I have written.

How the Lord miraculously provided the funds to print and distribute over 2 million newsletters is also an area I should mention since Christian Life Services does not solicit donations. The cost of distributing the newsletters so far amounts to several hundred thousand dollars. The Lord blessed the company I help manage, and the owner shared a portion of that success with me. He gave me a generous share of the company's stock. Pimalco's success made it an irresistible target for ownership and in 1985, the company reached an agreement with Alcoa, the leading aluminum company in the world, to sell a portion of its stock. This stock sale occurred a few months before I needed the large sums of money required to mail newsletters in volume, and it has provided most of the necessary funds over the past several years for distributing all of the newsletters at no charge. I have never taken any money personally for anything I have ever written including the book. As long as I am working, I can do this at no expense to the Body of Christ because the Lord has so generously supplied all of our needs through the means of my employment.

HOLY FEAR: A PERSONAL EXPERIENCE

I have given a part of our testimony for you to see how Barbara and I have walked by faith with a holy fear for the saving of our family in the end times. I am not saying that the same things that happened to us will happen to you if you have a fear of the Lord. I cannot say whether or not the Lord would want you to adopt a houseful of children, move across the country, start a school, write a book, or found a ministry. But I can promise you that the Holy Spirit can only go to work if your heart is right before God. If you are seeking the Lord's will regardless of personal cost, then you will experience the Lord's power in your life, whatever He has planned for you. In my case it began when the Lord showed me things about the Enemy's method of spiritual attack during the end times. My own revelation from the Lord came after a visit with my brother Charles in 1971 in which the Lord revealed the identity of the beast of Revelation 13.

It was this revelation that caused us, like Noah, to move with holy fear for the saving of our family. I have learned many things about our spiritual enemy and his end-time warfare from the Bible study and historical

research I've written about. But without the strong mortar of holy fear, the information from my study which
formed the building blocks would have had little
strength. It would not have held up to the Enemy's influence to compromise God's standards. The substance of
this revelation which brought about our walking with a
holy fear is discussed in the next chapter.

Chapter 3

THE REVELATION

Barbara and I would never have left our Ohio home had it not been for the revelation my brother Charles received. During June 1971, God revealed the identity of the beast described by the Apostle John in Revelation 13. Charles Fraley, now a missionary surgeon in Kenya, Africa, learned that the United States government becomes the beast-superpower of the last days and that the "wound of the beast" (Revelation 13:3) refers to the Japanese attack on Pearl Harbor in 1941. After Charles told me about this, I was motivated to spend thousands of hours of research to find out for myself whether or not this interpretation squared with the facts of history and agreed with prophetic Scripture. More than anything else, it was this revelation that identified the end-time beast, and that placed a holy fear within Barbara and me. We developed a deep reverence for God's holiness and a strong desire to do His will.

This chapter opens with a portion of an interview. Sid Roth, President of Messianic Vision, interviewed Charles and me for his national radio program in January 1988. In it, Charles describes the revelation in his own words and I discuss the outcome of my research. The remainder of the chapter chronicles the actual historical events and identifies the significance of the beast's wound.

––––––––––

SID ROTH: Dr. Fraley, you are now a missionary in Kenya, Africa. So that we can get to know you a little better—I understand that your whole life was transformed by a vision from God—tell us about that.

CHARLES FRALEY: Yes, Sid, I grew up in a family of thirteen children and I was number twelve. It seems that I've always had a desire to know God since I can remember. I came to know Christ as my Savior when I was eleven years old. Out of high school, I went into the Navy and it was there that God gave me a great desire to know Him through His Word. So I spent a great deal of time studying the Word of God, and during that time I was led to commit my life to the Lord Jesus Christ for His service and direction. About two years later, as I was praying, I had a vision one night where God instructed me to go into medicine, become a doctor, and become a medical missionary to Africa.

SID ROTH: Chuck, had you had many visions previous to that or was this a unique thing in your life?

CHARLES FRALEY: This was unique. The only, what I would call "supernatural experience" I had before that, was a couple of years before when I committed my life to Christ for His service. The presence of God surrounded me one day as I was reading Hebrews 13:5, and God spoke that Word to my spirit. It says, "Let your conversation be without covetousness and be content with such things as you have, for He hath said, 'Never will I leave you nor forsake you.'" That caused me to commit my life into the Lord's hands.

SID ROTH: So, what did you want to do from that vision of becoming a medical missionary?

CHARLES FRALEY: I said, "O.K. Lord, if that's what you

want me to do, I will do it." I did not know at that time what was required, or what it would involve.

SID ROTH: Had you had any thoughts of becoming a doctor?

CHARLES FRALEY: Never. It had never once entered my mind.

SID ROTH: Had you any thoughts of serving the Lord full-time in another country?

CHARLES FRALEY: I had some general thoughts that that could be possible. I would be willing to do it if God directed me that way.

SID ROTH: I understand that you became a doctor and promptly decided to be very content in this country, and not go to another land.

CHARLES FRALEY: Yes. By the time I was obedient to that directive and went into medical school, and went through thirteen years of training—eight years of college, one year as an intern and four years as a resident surgeon—I had slipped in my spiritual walk with the Lord. I had allowed thoughts to come into my mind that I could serve God just as well in this country, even though I had had a direct leading from the Lord to go elsewhere.

SID ROTH: How did you rationalize something like that?

CHARLES FRALEY: Well, it's hard to say. It developed sort of in a subtle way and just infiltrated my mind. I justified it on the idea that even though I was going to practice for a time in this country, I was still willing to go on overseas when the Lord showed me that I should do so. But I really was rationalizing at that point.

SID ROTH: How did this change?

CHARLES FRALEY: Well, after I was in practice for some time, I was brought to the point that I realized that I was not walking with God. That so hurt me and devastated me when I was shown that I had gotten away from the Lord—after having once committed myself to Him—

that I began to seek God for a new filling of the Holy Spirit and power to walk with Him through His will. And I put every ounce of my being into seeking God for seven months.

SID ROTH: Tell me how you did that. Did you work during this time?

CHARLES FRALEY: I continued to work. I spent almost all of my spare time in the Word of God, meditating, and praying, and just worshipped during that seven month period.

SID ROTH: And did you have anything as dramatic as that first call?

CHARLES FRALEY: Yes, I did. After that seven month period, I went on a two-week vacation which I spent in fasting and just seeking God, waiting on God, fully expecting to be filled in a new way with the power of the Holy Spirit. And it was after about ten days of that waiting on God at that time that I began to have visions and received this revelation, which I was not seeking. It came in a very unexpected way.

SID ROTH: You're talking about the revelation of the wound of the beast?

CHARLES FRALEY: Yes.

SID ROTH: Well, I guess that's as good an introduction as we can have. Tell us about that revelation.

CHARLES FRALEY: I was awakened one night, after ten days of seeking God, and knew the presence of someone there with me in a special way, and began to have visions. I first had a vision of a large, fat head of a beast, which was swallowing Christians up through materialism and pleasure. Then I had about five visions of Jesus. One was revealed that Jesus was a very disciplined person, who had His face set like a flint. Nothing could deviate him from His purpose in life. Another one was His great love for us. Another one was the tremendous price that He paid on the cross for our salvation. And, of course, through this, God was showing me how He did not deserve the kind of treatment that I had given Him in backing down from my original calling. Then the next morning, the Spirit of the Lord drew me very strongly to the book of Revelation. I had remembered something about a beast in the book of Revelation, and as I opened the pages and went through the book of Revelation, I came to the thirteenth chapter. And as I opened the page to this chapter, Revelation 13:3 just literally jumped right out of the book and seared itself into my mind. And I understood perfectly the fulfillment of this verse as if I had always known it.

SID ROTH: But, the truth of the matter is that this was all brand new to you?

CHARLES FRALEY: Brand new. I had never once heard this kind of interpretation of this verse.

SID ROTH: This was Revelation 13:3. I'm reading the New King James translation: "I saw one of his heads as if it had been mortally wounded and his deadly wound was healed, and all the world marvelled and followed the beast." And God gave you a revelation of what the wound of this beast was?

CHARLES FRALEY: Yes, it was revealed that the fulfillment of this verse, which had been written 2,000 years ago, took place at Pearl Harbor in 1941.

SID ROTH: Pearl Harbor?

CHARLES FRALEY: Yes.

SID ROTH: Did you have problems accepting this or was this truth to you? Because I can tell you that I have personally been to Pearl Harbor and I mean that was a horrible thing that occurred, but that doesn't seem that significant as the way the Bible describes it here. It's [the beast] mortally wounded?

CHARLES FRALEY: Yes. I had several problems with this. It came as quite a shock. One problem that I had was the fact that I had always been taught that the book of Revelation was not to take place until some time in the future. Specifically, until after we were raptured. So I really wasn't too concerned with it. If this were true, the book of Revelation was already taking place and some of it was already history, including this particular verse. Another shock was that if this were true, the beast mentioned in Revelation 13 was indeed our own empire, the United States government. And this was very hard for me to accept.

SID ROTH: Why?

CHARLES FRALEY: Because I had always been taught that it was to be a particular man or person that was to rise up and rule the world, and perhaps he might be associated with the European economic community, but I never associated the United States as being a major part of this development.

SID ROTH: What did you do with this tremendous revelation? I mean, obviously God gave it to you for a reason. What did you do with it?

CHARLES FRALEY: Well, I resisted it for the first few days, but I could absolutely get no peace until I accepted the fact that this was true. But the thing it made me do was realize how short the time is, that we were in a period of time when the time was short, and I began to realize that it was very important that I get my commitment with the Lord straight.

SID ROTH: And that verse again is, "I saw one of his heads as if it had been mortally wounded, and his deadly wound was healed and all the world marvelled and followed the beast." Now you had never thought of that as being Pearl Harbor, and, therefore, the beast is who?

CHARLES FRALEY: This meant that the beast had to be the United States government.

SID ROTH: But wait a second, and I am going to have to direct this question to Bob Fraley—I have to tell you, logically, when I hear "Pearl Harbor," I do not equate that to a mortal wounding of the United States of America. I equate it to something horrible that occurred, but not to a mortal wounding. To me that's more significant. How would you respond?

BOB FRALEY: Sid, after my brother, Dr. Fraley, shared this revelation with me, I was literally driven by the Spirit of the Lord to prove it to be true or false through biblical research and historical study. I had to know. Maybe it was my analytical way of thinking that wanted the facts—one way or the other.

To properly answer your question about equating the attack on Pearl Harbor as a mortal wounding of the United States, I need to back up, and first make some preliminary comments. In Revelation 13:1, John states that this beast that he saw had seven heads, and then here in Revelation 13:3, he states *only one* of these heads was mortally wounded. In my research and word studies of the prophetic words used by John in these verses to describe this beast, I found the word "head" means leadership. I discovered the use of the word for the numeral seven means "complete." The word "seven" throughout Scripture is used to indicate something being complete, such as it took seven days for the creation. Of course, anyone can check on what I am saying and research the meaning of these words.

The word "beast," I found in the book of Daniel, refers to a government superpower. In biblical times they called leading world powers "empires," but today we call them "superpowers." In Revelation 13:1, John says he saw this beast coming up out of the sea. Both Scripture and history show this phrase has reference to a world superpower made up of people from many different countries, laws, and customs. So when John makes reference to a beast with seven heads in Revelation Chapter 13, he is prophetically describing a government superpower in the end time that will be complete in its leadership. Prophetically the word *beast* means superpower; *seven* means complete; *heads* means leadership.

For a government system to be complete in its world leadership position would mean that it would have to be number one in all phases of leading world indicators. Our particular governmental system does meet those qualifications. In fact, we are the only government system in the world today that qualifies to be prophetically described as having "seven heads."

We are number one, not just in military strength, for example, but we also have been number one in political power, economics, industrial output, agricultural output, commerce, manufacturing of goods and services, and all other areas. We are the leader in all areas of the world system. That is why when John saw into the last days, and saw our particular governmental system, the Spirit of the Lord led him to use the phrase "seven heads" in describing our world leadership position.

Now, Sid, with my brief review of what I believe to be some important and necessary facts about what John is discussing in this prophecy, I can more clearly answer your questions about the bombing of Pearl Harbor, and why it can be considered a mortal wound to one of our heads—our military leadership. I have researched what the historians had to say about Japan's bombing of Pearl Harbor. There are many well-written books documenting all the historical events and records that surrounded that attack, what led up to it, the attack itself and how totally devastating it was. One interesting fact I found about this event, is that one of the main objectives of the Commander of the Japanese naval forces was to *mortally wound* our military capabilities.

SID ROTH: He actually uses that terminology?

BOB FRALEY: He uses that term. We could better understand why, if we go back in time to when Pearl Harbor took place. In those days, 1941, what qualified you as a world military leader was your naval force. Your naval power.

SID ROTH: It's like today we look at the Air Force.

BOB FRALEY: That's right! In the 30's and 40's, it was a country's naval fleet that was the significant military mode of power. And the most significant part of your naval force, in those days, was your battleships. According to what the historians say about that time, and the way the military people evaluated the importance of battleships, the loss of one battleship would have almost been considered devastating. In the bombing of Pearl Harbor, eight of our battleships were sunk or suffered significant damage. That was unthinkable. That would definitely be classified as a mortal wound to our military head, which is what John saw through his prophetic eyes. A significant point should be made here in order to properly understand this prophecy. John does not say the entire beast (leadership of the American government) was mortally wounded. He says *only one* of its heads was wounded.

SID ROTH: In other words, Japan felt if they could pull this off, they could cause a mortal blow to America. Was it their goal to take over America?

BOB FRALEY: Not according to my studies. Although historians indicate most of the world concluded our military head [leadership] had received a mortal wound beyond recovery, the Japanese did not pursue their first attack. Their real objective was more in their own geographical area. Japan was expanding their military possessions in their part of the world of Southeast Asia. But they knew the one thing that stood between them and their taking over Indo-China, the Philippines, and other countries in their sector of the world was the Pacific Fleet of the United States Navy stationed at Pearl Harbor. This was the greatest battle force located anywhere in the world. It was intimidating to the Japanese military efforts, and acted like a thorn in the flesh of their objectives.

CHARLES FRALEY: Another thing that has interested me since that time of the revelation as a physician and surgeon, is the fact that I was always taught, and therefore thought, that this mortal wound was referring to a man.

SID ROTH: Most people think that.

CHARLES FRALEY: And yet I see now in my own experience, I have been able to bring many people back to life who received mortal wounds. And this particular statement has lost a lot of its meaning through medical science, if it just referred to a man.

SID ROTH: Bob, in your book, you outline where Scripture refers to the "beast" with the pronoun "he." It really should be according to the proper Greek, translated, I believe, the pronoun "it."

BOB FRALEY: Yes. There are some translations, the King James and New International Version, for example, that translate the pronoun in Revelation 13, which refers to the beast, with the English word "he," "his," or "him."

SID ROTH: So you think of that as being a person?

BOB FRALEY: Yes, that would certainly seem to be the proper conclusion. However, other translations, the Revised Standard Version, for example, do not translate this pronoun as "he," which implies the beast is a man, but translates this pronoun "it" which implies the beast is a system or government as you find in the book of Daniel. Because of this discrepancy in the various translations, I had to research the scholars to find which is the correct translation. This was critical in view of my brother's revelation.

The Greek word *autou* is the pronoun which makes reference to the beast throughout Revelation 13. We know a pronoun should always carry the same gender as that noun to which it refers. Throughout chapter 13, this pronoun refers to the Greek noun *therion* which is the Greek word for "beast." Interestingly enough, I found the gender of this Greek noun used for beast is not masculine, but neuter. Therefore, translating the pronoun with the words, "he," "his," or "him," which is masculine gender is incorrect. The pronoun which makes reference to the beast in Revelation 13 should be translated "it" which is neuter. Translating the gender incorrectly by using the words "he," "his," or "him" certainly could cause us to assume the word beast refers to some man. Up until now, very few people would have ever had a reason to question this area even though various Bible translations differ.

You will be interested to know that Charles Fraley continues to serve as a surgeon in East Africa. He works under the auspices of African Inland Mission. He is currently the missionary medical coordinator for African Inland Church in Kenya. Charles is responsible for two major hospitals, four smaller hospitals, and about 45 clinics/dispensaries throughout the country. His field address is:

> Dr. Charles Fraley
> A.I.C. Medical Coordinator
> Box 21010, Nairobi
> Kenya, East Africa

REMEMBER PEARL HARBOR

President Bush journeyed to Hawaii December 7, 1991, to revisit Pearl Harbor on the 50th Anniversary of the Japanese attack. Historians, statesmen and journalists throughout the world refer to this attack as one of the greatest turning points in world history. At the time, the world viewed the event as a mortal wound to U.S. military leadership.

But this event jarred the United States into astonishing activity like no other. The "day of infamy" was the catalytic event of the century. As U.S. soldiers marched off to war, the duties of men and women greatly expanded. Indeed, the Second World War set into motion forces that changed forever the way Americans work, play, build families, and conduct their lives. The war transformed our land from a provincial, isolationist country to a superpower, a technological hothouse of incredible economic, political, and military power. We shared this superpower role with the Soviet Union until its recent breakup. *Now the United States stands alone.* Never before has one nation achieved such undisputable dominance.

Pearl Harbor has had tremendous significance for the course of human history, but it has even greater significance to those who are following Jesus Christ. This landmark event that encompassed so much was prophesied by John in the book of Revelation. Knowing its place in Bible prophecy is one of the major keys to our understanding the spiritual war during the last days of the Church Age.

THE WOUND OF THE BEAST

As I mentioned to Sid Roth during the interview, I have reviewed several books and documentaries about Japan's bombing of Pearl Harbor. If what Charles was saying about the wound of the beast and the attack on Pearl Harbor were true, it must square with the facts of history. And so I have read widely about the Japanese in Pearl Harbor that day.

In my effort to find the historical significance of what happened that December morning, I discovered one account that stands head and shoulders above all the others. *At Dawn We Slept,* by Gordon W. Prange, is considered the finest historical work on the topic.[1] This book has been praised by historians and publishers as a "masterpiece" and as "authoritative," "unparalleled," "definitive," and "impossible to forget."

Prange was uniquely qualified for his task. He was educated at the University of Iowa and the University of Berlin. Later, he taught history at the University of Maryland. From October 1946 to June 1951, Prange was chief of General Douglas MacArthur's G-2 Historical Section located at General HQ, Far East Command, Tokyo. From his historical training and firsthand knowledge, he knew more about the Japanese attack on Pearl Harbor than any other person. He interviewed virtually every surviving Japanese officer who took part in the Pearl Harbor operation, as well as every pertinent source on the U.S. side. His 873-page history of the attack is based on 37 years of research. It's acclaimed world-wide; it's without equal. In my own study of the attack, I found it to be an invaluable reference.

Prelude to Pearl Harbor

The Japanese attack on Pearl Harbor is easily one of the most significant naval operations in twentieth-century military history. But it was even more than that—it was one of the turning points in modern world history. It was so sudden, so unexpected, so spectacular, so devastating. So much happened that day—militarily, politically, and psychologically—that much of it seems inexplicable and mysterious. Many people who lived through the 1940s tend to divide their lives into two periods—before Pearl Harbor, and after Pearl Harbor. The U.S. Congress convened a joint committee to investigate the event, and the committee filled forty volumes with its findings. Military historians agree that the Japanese attack on Pearl Harbor was the greatest defeat any nation had ever suffered at the beginning of a war.

It's difficult to exaggerate the importance of naval power to national security prior to the Nuclear Age. During the 1940s and earlier, most Americans believed, as did people throughout the industrialized world, that ships were the ultimate technological achievement. Battleships were the mightiest weapons of war, and luxury liners represented the epitome of western culture. When a great ship went down—the *Lusitania,* the *Bismarck,* or the *Titanic*—people listened to the details in horror. Sinking ships were cataclysmic events akin to natural disasters like earthquakes and hurricanes.

In the spring of 1940, a large segment of America's Pacific Fleet had been stationed at Pearl Harbor. It was the world's greatest aggregation of warships—a million tons of fighting steel—and it secured the western front of our mighty nation.

U.S. influence in the Pacific irritated the Japanese. Japan feared that America's huge naval program would blot out the Rising Sun. The Pacific Fleet stood directly in the way of Japan's ambitious career of conquest in the 1930s. While the European nations fought each other, Japan built its empire in Southeast Asia. The island nation could not miss this golden opportunity.

So, in December 1940, Admiral Isoroku Yamamoto, Commander-in-Chief of Japan's combined fleet, decided to launch a surprise attack at Pearl Harbor. He planned for the attack to come at the outset of war with the United States. If Japan were to achieve political supremacy in the Pacific, it would have to neutralize America's military capacity. Yamamoto knew that just as a weaker judo expert can toss a stronger opponent by catching him off balance, Japan would have to seize the initiative for the island nation to defeat the United States. By knocking out the U.S. Pacific Fleet in one bold stroke, Yamamoto hoped to gain the edge in military strength for a year. He and his advisors concluded that Japan could best achieve an early decisive engagement with the U.S. Navy by bringing the scene of action to the waters of the Hawaiian Islands.

Yamamoto caught the United States sleeping—literally. The United States' perspective prior to the attack can best be summed up by a statement made on February 19, 1941, by Congressman Charles I. Faddis of Pennsylvania. He declared,

> The Japanese are not going to risk a fight with a first class nation. They are unprepared to do so, and no one knows better than they do. They will not dare to get into a position where they must face the American Navy in open battle. Their Navy is not strong enough and their homeland is too vulnerable.

It took a year of intense preparation for the Japanese naval forces to be ready. All of the planning had to be done in the strictest secrecy. The attack would have to catch the United States by surprise or it would fail. Japanese military planners had to solve several problems in order to launch the attack. They designed torpedoes capable of operating in the shallow waters of Pearl Harbor; they produced new armor-piercing shells that could be delivered by planes from low altitudes; they selected pilots and trained them to fly in an area like Pearl Harbor. The Japanese also had to organize the task force, learn how to refuel the ships in the rough northern Pacific Ocean—the route selected to avoid detection. They chose the best day and time for the attack to assure a complete surprise. The Pearl Harbor plan was the most highly-classified, closely-guarded, best-kept secret of World War II.

At 6 o'clock on the morning of November 26, 1941, the Japanese strike force weighed anchor. Twelve days later, they reached the launching point for their attack: 230 miles due north of the island of Oahu, Hawaii. It was just

before dawn on December 7. The Japanese force of 33
warships included six aircraft carriers that had success-
fully sailed on a northern route through rough waters
and dense fog to avoid detection by American ships and
surveillance aircraft.

The Attack

War! It came with startling swiftness that Sunday
morning. On every Japanese carrier, the scene was the
same. The engines sputtered to life, up fluttered the signal flag, then down again, and one by one, the aircraft
roared down the flight decks drowning the cheers and
yells from the crews. Plane after plane rose, flashing in
the early morning sun that peeked over the horizon. This
airborne armada consisted of 353 planes. It represented
the largest concentration of air power in the history of
warfare. On the island of Oahu, American sailors were
unaware of the tremendous fighting force that would
send many of them to a watery grave.

Perfect timing was essential. The Japanese knew full
well that if anything went wrong, the entire surprise
attack would collapse. They were now dead on course.
Their mission: destruction of the U.S. Pacific Fleet at
Pearl Harbor and all of the nearby American Air Force
installations.

It was 7:40 AM when the first Japanese pilots sighted
Oahu's coastline—still undetected. The element of surprise belonged to the Japanese. Even the weather
favored their mission. The mountain pass northwest of
the harbor is almost always cloud-covered. But the one
day a year, it is said, the pass is clear happened to be
that Sunday morning. This meant that the Japanese
attack planes could fly through the pass without being
spotted. As the first wave came through the pass, they
deployed into three groups. The planes struck Hickam

Air Force Base, Wheeler Field, Bellows Field, Kaneohe Naval Base and the Naval Air Station at Ford Island. At 7:55 the devastating assault began.

At Wheeler Field, a long row of hangars and fighters invited the Japanese. The enemy planes bombed the hangars and strafed the quarter mile row of planes drawn up outside. Wheeler Field was levelled in minutes.

The method of attack on each air field was the same— up and back, up and back. Flying at tree-top level, successive waves of Japanese aircraft skimmed in, attacking, strafing then wheeling around to return again and again. Since all of the air bases were so close together, the attacks all came at the same time. Everything happened at once.

The attacks were devastating. Hangars were burned, barracks were razed, and hundreds of men were killed. A total of 341 U.S. planes were destroyed or damaged on the ground that Sunday morning. Very few American fighters were able to get airborne to counterattack.

But the assault on the air fields was only the beginning of the Pearl Harbor drama. Mitsuo Fuchida, the Japanese commander who led the first formation of planes, later wrote, "The harbor was still asleep in the morning mist." Inside that sleeping harbor were 96 warships of the United States Pacific Fleet. They included 8 cruisers, 29 destroyers, 5 submarines, assorted mine craft and 8 U.S. battleships: the *USS West Virginia, USS Arizona, USS Oklahoma, USS Nevada,* the *Tennessee,* the *Pennsylvania,* the *California* and *USS Maryland.*

Dive bombers rocked the harbor. They scored 19 direct hits. The mammoth gray ships along Battleship Row, writhing from the explosions of bombs and torpedoes, burned at their moorings, sending billows of black smoke into the morning skies over the island of Oahu. They dealt crippling blows to ship after ship. Most of the damage was done in the first fifteen minutes.

The attack on Pearl Harbor ended about 9:45 AM. In one hour and fifty minutes, the Japanese immobilized almost the entire air strength of Oahu, and nearly eliminated their chief objective, the U.S. Pacific Fleet. The once-mighty U.S. military fortress at Oahu had been pulverized. As the drone of enemy formations disappeared over the horizon heading back to their carriers, they left behind a scene of horrible chaos—crackling flames, moaning men, and hissing steam. Half-submerged ships were strewn about the harbor, tilting at crazy angles. Wreckage floated across the oily surface of the water as bodies washed ashore.

Nineteen ships, including eight battleships, were sunk or heavily damaged. The battleship *California,* alone at the southern end of Battleship Row caught the first of two torpedoes at 8:05 AM. After two additional bomb hits, she went down and settled on the bottom of the harbor. The battleship *West Virginia* was hit by six torpedoes and two bombs, and slowly she joined the *California.* The battleship *Oklahoma* received five torpedo hits in the very first minutes. By 8:30 she had rolled completely over and lay like an enormous whale revealing her briny propellers. Huge geysers burst forth from the battleship *Nevada* as a result of bombings. She was on fire and her hull showed a series of gaping holes. The battleship *Utah,* struck by three aerial torpedoes was sunk forever. The battleship *Pennsylvania,* the Pacific Fleet Flagship, had been in dry dock undergoing repairs along with two destroyers, the *Cassin* and *Downes.* All three took bomb hits. The *Pennsylvania* was not damaged beyond repair, but the *Cassin* and *Downes* were so completely wrecked they had to be scrapped.

Meanwhile, the destroyer *Shaw* staggered under three bomb hits, one of them rupturing her fuel tanks. In the dramatic explosion, the whole harbor was transfixed by a blinding blast of heat and light. The explosion ripped off her bow and sank the ship and the dry dock as well.

The battleship *Arizona* was sunk by a single 1760 pound armor-piercing action bomb. The bomb penetrated through six decks of steel and exploded in the main aviation fuel storage tank. A tremendous internal chain reaction followed. The force of the explosion was so great it raised the bow of the ship completely out of the water, and split her right behind the number one gun turret. The *Arizona* sank in less than nine minutes. Out of her crew of 1,543 men, 1,177 lost their lives in those few awful minutes.

USS Arizona

The Arizona Memorial

Today, the *USS Arizona* rests peacefully in an upright position under 38 feet of water at the bottom of Pearl Harbor. The years have slipped by quickly and the scars of the attack have all but been forgotten by most Americans. However, the stark horror and grim reminder of that Sunday morning which caught the country in the fierce vortex of history will live forever through the Arizona Memorial, dedicated on Memorial Day, 1962. Oil still rises from the rusting hull of the *USS Arizona,* and the 1,100 men still entombed there mirror the most eloquent witness to the fury of defeat on Pearl Harbor Day.

Arizona Memorial Spans Sunken USS Arizona

It is astounding to discover that the theme of the design used for building this memorial reflects the prophecy given by John in Revelation 13:3. John said, "One of the heads of the beast seemed to have had a fatal wound, but the fatal wound had been healed." The form of this memorial was structurally designed with a sag in the center to express the initial defeat of America (which appeared to be a fatal wound to our military head), but stands strong and vigorous at the ends—to express eventual victory.

This colossal victory of having executed the attack on Pearl Harbor with surprise belonged to Japan, but the greatest defeat in America's history aroused the fighting spirit of Americans everywhere. Over the next 42 months, America forged the greatest warpower the world has ever known and won wars on two widely separated fronts, Asia and Europe, while our own homeland remained untouched. The whole world was awestruck by the way the United States demonstrated its great power and ended the war with the dropping of the atomic bomb. "The fatal wound had indeed been healed," as stated by John in Revelation 13:3 .

Arizona Memorial Design Theme

BABYLON REVISITED

Please understand what Charles and I are saying. In stating that the United States government is the beast of Revelation 13, we are not suggesting that Americans should not love their country or pray for government leaders. Quite the contrary, in no way do I want to take away from the great spiritual history of this nation.

The Apostle John uses the term "beast" in Revelation to indicate a dominant world government just like the Bible uses the term "beast" in other places to describe dominant world powers. Just as Paul instructed Christians to pray for the leaders of the Roman government in his day, we are to do the same for our government. I believe that we in the church have often built up the beast of Revelation to be some kind of detestable monster. In prophetic Scripture, the word "beast" simply means something mighty and powerful. One of its uses in Scripture is to refer to a government superpower like the Roman Empire or the United States.

It's easy to forget that Jesus was born under a government system called a "beast" in Scripture—the Roman government. The church began under a government system called a "beast" in Scripture. The American church—the center of Christianity during the the final days of the Church Age—is also under a superpower-government system called a "beast" in Scripture. John warns that Satan will use this end-time beast-system to attack the saints (Revelation 12:17). Recognizing that the United States government is the beast calls for concern about this nation's moral deterioration, not sedition or anarchy. It may hurt our pride as American citizens, but Christians must accept the fact that many Americans lead immoral lives today.

Satan has worked through our government's law making power in recent years to wipe out Christian standards. He has removed the reverence for the laws of God within society. As a result, the values that shaped American lives for centuries have eroded in a single generation. The unthinkable has become normal. The majority of our society has lost the ability to discern right from wrong. The subject of walking before the Lord in holy fear is almost unheard of today, even within churches.

In the Bible, the beast is associated with Babylon. In Revelation 18 and parts of Jeremiah 50 and 51, God tells us about the counsel He has taken against a certain Babylon at the close of the Gentile Age. I think you will agree that what is said of the biblical Babylon can be fairly said of American society today:

— "The youngest of the nations" (Jeremiah 50:12)
— "Born from a mother country" (50:12)
— "A mighty military and political power" (50:23)
— "An arrogant, proud, and haughty nation" (50:31)

— "People of foreign descent" (50:37)
— "Covetousness reigns as the people live sumptuously, but want more while many in the world are starving" (50:38)
— "Nation with Godly heritage" (51:7)
— "A nation of great wealth and prosperity" (51:13)
— "Great attainments" (51:33)
— "Space traveler" (51:53)
— "A home for the cults and occult practices" (Revelation 18:2)
— "Worldwide immorality" (18:2)
— "Large in foreign aid" (18:3)
— "Large importer to satisfy the lust of the people" (18:3)
— "Center of Christianity" (18:4)
— "Sins piled to heaven" (18:5)
— "Proud and boastful people" (18:7)
— "Other countries economic strength depends on her economic strength" (18:9-19)
— "World trade center" (18:11-13)
— "Extravagant tastes" (18:4)
— "Nation of influential cities" (18:18)
— "Nation known for her music" (18:22)
— "Nation known for her manufacturing capabilities" (18:22)
— "Nation known for her food production" (18:22)
— "Her businessmen and great corporations are known worldwide" (18:23).

The revelation Charles received concerning the identity of the beast has not been easy to defend because it challenges traditional eschatology, that is, the doctrine of last things. And believe me, I have nothing to gain personally by sharing its message. It would have been much easier and less costly for me to forget about it. But Barbara and I believe the Lord has not given us that choice.

We have an obligation to report the revelation, not to make people believe it. So I invite you to consider its message. The rest is between you and the Lord. This revelation helped us understand the nature of spiritual warfare in these last days. It set our family's course and produced the holy fear that has guided our path.

AMERICA AS THE BEAST

So what does it mean to say that the United States governmental system is the beast of Revelation that appears near the end of the Church Age? Twenty years after I began my study of Charles's revelation, I can tell you it means that *Satan has declared war on America.* Satan aims to harm as many people as possible. He has undertaken an all-out offensive on this nation, its people, and their spiritual heritage. The prophecy concerning the beast is being fulfilled. American society as we know it today will fall as described in Revelation 14:8 and 18:10, 17.

Does that mean that World War III is around the corner, that foreign terrorists will seize control of the government, or that Christians in America will be openly persecuted for their faith? Outright persecution may happen at some point in the future, but Satan's primary method of warfare at this time is *deception,* not *persecution.* America's spiritual downfall is being brought about by its own hand, not some foreign army. Our government is playing a major role as Satan's ally by erasing many of the laws that formed the moral foundations of American society. Daniel prophesied this would happen (Daniel 7:25). This is how Satan has worked through our government leaders to destroy respect for God's standards. The last battle for America's spiritual heritage will be waged by seducing spirits.

Chapter 4

SEDUCING SPIRITS

Living within the beast-system is a sobering thought. The Apostle John, as well as Paul in his letter to Timothy (2 Timothy 3:1-5), tell us that this time will be very difficult for Christians. John says that the beast was given power "to make war with the saints and to overcome them" (Revelation 13:7). To "overcome" the saints means that Satan's influence will be so great that many Christians will no longer lead a Christian life of victory in marriage, family, work, and everyday activities. Satan will sap Christians power and trample over them in their weakened condition.

In 1965 the Lord revealed, through the writings of a contemporary prophet, spiritual insight into the beast's method of "making war" on the saints. More than twenty years later I first read this message, and through it God showed me that recognizing the work of "seducing spirits" is critical to the Christian's survival in these times. In this chapter, I present the solemn prophetic warning that describes seducing spirits activities. The prophetic warning describes the demonic forces campaign of distortion and deception, and it contains the Lord's message to His people. But first, a few words about how I came into possession of this prophetic warning.

THE SEARCH FOR THE MISSING PROPHET

Over the years I have received quantities of material from people throughout the country—throughout the world really. People influenced by my book, *The Last Days in America,* or one of my newsletters have sent letters, articles, pictures, and other items. While I share the prayer requests with Christian friends, I simply do not have time to read all printed material that comes in because I have so many other responsibilities.

Ten years ago or so, I received a large envelope from Shirley Christianson of Prescott, Arizona. In her letter, she explained that she had been a believer for many years and that she had written a number of articles. She believed she should send me the materials enclosed— there were articles, poems, and clippings of various kinds—and that I would know what to do with them. I gave her a call and discovered that she was a dear sister in the Lord. I told her I didn't know when I could get to her articles, and they were stored away in a cabinet with materials sent in by hundreds of others.

Then in March, 1987 I awoke at 4 o'clock in the morning. I received a divine word from the Lord within my spirit that I was to retrieve Shirley Christianson's materials. As I shuffled through the cabinet full of papers, I came across the little bundle she had sent. One of the writings stood out from all the others. No author, no title could be found. At that moment I did not even know the document contained an end-times prophecy. I just knew that what was written on those pieces of paper was from the Lord.

After reading the document several times, I decided to have it typed. I made copies for a group of Christians attending a retreat with Barbara and me that weekend. Together, we discussed the manuscript and agreed that it was a timely message from the Lord. After the retreat, I mentioned to Barbara that I planned to distribute the prophecy to those on the Christian Life newsletter mailing list. She thought it was certainly worthy of publication, but she suggested that I find out who wrote it first. I thought her advice was really a word of wisdom. She said it was a matter of common sense.

So my search for the author began. I tried to contact Shirley Christianson but learned that she had passed away. I surmised that she had written the prophecy, but I could not be certain. Because I had nothing to go on except the original pages, I began to wonder if I would ever find the missing prophet.

A month passed. A good friend, Pat O'Shell offered to help read some of the mail I had received. She and her husband, Hal planned to spend a few weeks with their daughter Cathy in San Francisco, so she took along a stack. "You're not going to believe this," she said on the phone one day, "but there is a letter here from a man in Arkansas. Along with his letter is a paper that contains about half of that prophetic message we discussed at our recent retreat." She mailed me the letter, and I made a call to Arkansas. I was excited because the Lord had opened a channel for me to continue my search.

The Arkansas connection was only the beginning. The contact there knew nothing about the prophecy's origin; he received it from a friend in San Diego. I called the friend, and he did not know where the prophecy had come from either, only that an elderly Christian man in San Diego made a point of sharing it with others. I contacted this man. He was a retired missionary who maintained regular contact with over a hundred missionaries overseas. He knew that the life of a foreign missionary could be lonely at times so he sent news and encouragement. When I explained why I had called, his voice grew excited. Not only did he know who had written the message, he knew the author personally.

He told me the prophecy was given by Stanley Frodsham. Brother Frodsham had given the message in 1965 at a Chicago meeting. Frodsham himself had died in 1971, but during his life he was known as "The Writing Prophet." For many years, Frodsham edited *Evangel Magazine,* an official monthly publication of the Assembly of God denomination. Frodsham's life and ministry is described in a biography entitled *Stanley Frodsham: Prophet With A Pen.*[1]

Frodsham's prophecy was published by Christian Life Services in the June 1987 newsletter. It is reprinted here, in its entirety.

A SOLEMN PROPHETIC WARNING

It is written: "Despise not prophesyings. Prove all things; hold fast that which is good" (I Thessalonians 5:20,21 KJV). The following are excerpts from prophetic words given to one who was under a heavy anointing. We believe all who read these solemn prophetic warnings should take diligent heed to them. "Believe in the Lord your God, so ye shall be established; believe His prophets, so shall ye prosper" (II Chronicles 20:20 KJV).

Great darkness is coming upon the countries that have heard My gospel but no longer walk in it. My wrath shall be manifested against all ungodliness. It shall come with great intensity. My judgments are literal, and not a thing to be lightly passed over. Before I visit the nations in judgment, I will begin at My house. When I do cause My wrath to come upon the cities of the world, My people shall be separate. I desire a people without spot or wrinkle, and such shall be preserved by Me in the time of My wrath coming upon all iniquity and unrighteousness.

I am going to prepare you for the coming days by a hard path that will cause you to cry out continually unto Me. For when the going is easy, men do not seek Me, but rejoice in a temporary blessing. And when that blessing is removed, they so often turn this way and that way, but do not come to Me. I am showing you these things that you may seek Me continually and with great diligence. As you seek Me, I will open up truths to you that you have not seen before, truths that will enable you to stand in the last days.

Coming Glory and Deceiving Spiritis

When I visit My people in mighty revival power it is to prepare them for the darkness ahead. With the glory shall come great darkness, for the glory is to prepare My people for the darkness. I will enable My people to go through because of the visitation of My Spirit. Take heed to yourselves lest ye be puffed up and think that you have arrived. Listen to the messengers, but do not hold man's persons in admiration. For many whom I shall anoint mightily with signs and miracles shall become lifted up and shall fall by the wayside. I do not do this willingly; I have made provision that they might stand. I call many into this ministry and equip them, but remember that many shall fall. They shall be like bright lights, and the people shall delight in them. But they shall be taken over by deceiving spirits, and shall lead many of My people astray.

Hearken diligently concerning these things, for in the last days shall come seducing spirits (I Timothy 4:1) that shall turn many of My anointed ones away. Many shall fall through divers lusts and because of sin abounding. But if you will seek Me diligently I will put My Spirit within you (Ezekiel 36:27). When one shall turn to the right hand or to the left hand, you shall not turn with them, but keep your eyes wholly on the Lord. The coming days are the most dangerous, difficult and dark, but there shall be a mighty outpouring of My Spirit upon many cities; and many shall be destroyed. My people must be diligently warned concerning the days that are ahead. Many shall turn after seducing spirits; many are already seducing My people. It is those who do righteousness that are righteous. Many cover sins by great theological words, but I warn you of seducing spirits who instruct My people in an evil way.

Many shall come with seducing spirits and hold out lustful enticements. You will find that after I have visited My people again, the way shall become more and more narrow, and fewer shall walk therein. But, be not deceived, the ways of righteousness are My ways. For though Satan come as an angel of light (II Corinthians 11:13-15), hearken not to him; for those who perform miracles and speak not righteousness are not of Me. I warn you with great intensity that I am going to judge My house and have a church without spot or wrinkle when I come. I desire to open your eyes and give you spiritual understanding that you may not be deceived, but may walk in uprightness of heart before Me, loving righteousness and hating every evil way. Look unto Me, and I will make you to perceive with the eyes of the Spirit the things that lurk in darkness, that are not visible to the human eye. Let Me lead you in this way that you may perceive the powers of darkness and battle against them. It is not a battle against flesh and blood, for if you battle in that way, you accomplish nothing. But if you let Me take over and battle against the powers of darkness, then they are defeated; and then liberation is brought to My people.

The Way of Deceivers

I warn you to search the Scriptures diligently concerning these last days, for the things that are written shall indeed be made manifest. There shall come deceivers among My people in increasing number, who shall speak forth the truth and shall gain the favor of the people, for the people shall examine the Scriptures and say, "What these men say is true." Then when they have gained the hearts of the people, then and then only shall they bring out these wrong doctrines. Therefore, I say that you should not give your hearts to men, nor hold people's persons in admiration. For by these very persons shall Satan enter into My people. Watch for seducers (II Timothy 3:13). Do you think a seducer will brandish a new heresy and flaunt it before the people? He will speak the words of righteousness and truth and will appear as a minister of light, declaring the Word. The people's hearts shall be won; they will bring out their doctrines, and the people shall be deceived. The people shall say, "Did he not speak thus and thus? And did we not examine it from the Word? Therefore he is a minister of righteousness. That he has now spoken we do not see in the Word, but it must be right, for the other things he spoke were true."

Be not deceived, for the deceiver will first work to gain the hearts of many and then shall bring forth his insidious doctrines. You cannot discern those who are of Me and those who are not of Me when they start to preach. But seek Me constantly, and then when these doctrines are brought out, you shall have a witness in your heart that these are not of Me. Fear not, for I have warned you. Many will be deceived, but if you walk in holiness and uprightness before the Lord, your eyes shall be opened, and the Lord will protect you. If you will constantly look unto the Lord, you will know when the doctrine changes, and you will not be brought into it. If your heart is right, I will keep you, and if you will look constantly to Me, I will uphold you.

The minister of righteousness shall be on this wise: his life shall agree with the Word, and his lips shall give forth that which is wholly true, and it will be no mixture. When the mixture appears, then you will know he is not a minister of righteousness. The deceivers speak first the truth and then error to cover their own sins, which they love. Therefore, I exhort and command you to study the Scriptures relative to seducing spirits, for this is one of the great dangers of these last days.

I desire you to be firmly established in My Word, and not in the personalities of men, that you will not be moved as so many shall be moved. I would keep you in the paths of righteousness. Take heed to yourselves, and follow not the seducing spirits that are already manifesting themselves. Diligently inquire of Me when you hear something that you have not seen in the Word, and do not hold people's persons in admiration, for it is by this very method that Satan will hold many of My people.

The Way of Triumph

I have come that you might have life and have it more abundantly, that you may triumph where I triumphed. On the cross I triumphed over all the powers of Satan, and I have called you to walk the same path. It is when your life is on the cross that you shall know the victory that I have experienced. As you are on the cross and seated in Me, then you shall know the power of the resurrection. When I come in My glory, the principalities and powers in the heavenly places shall be broken. Fret not, for I have given you power whereby you may tread down the powers of darkness and come forth victoriously. It was on the cross that I triumphed over all the powers of the enemy. My life shall flow through you as you enter into these precious truths. Look unto Me, and appropriate My life. As your eyes and desires are toward Me, and you know what it is to be crucified with Me, then you shall live, and your anointing shall increase. It was not in My life that I walked upon the earth, but it was in My life when I was upon the cross that I openly spoiled principalities and powers (Colossians 2:15).

I am showing you truth that shall cause you to overcome, to have power over the wicked one—truth that will liberate you and those around you. You shall know also the fellowship of My sufferings. There is no other way whereby you may partake of this heavenly glory and reign with Me. "If we suffer, we shall reign with Him" (II Timothy 2:12 KJV). I desire to make these truths real within you. As you keep them before you, you will liberate many who are in bondage. You will have revelations of those in darkness and will have the keys to liberate the captives. Many seek to liberate, but they have not the keys. Upon the cross continually you will know the power of My resurrection that you may also partake of My glory. As you are willing to walk with Me and rejoice in your sufferings, you shall partake of My glory. Look unto Me, for ye have need of power to overcome the wicked one and the bondage in other lives.

If you will indeed judge yourself, you shall not be judged (I Corinthians 11:31). As you seek My face and desire to be cleansed by Me in all truth and sincerity of heart, I will judge you in the secret place, and the things that are in the secret place of your heart shall not be made manifest to others. I will do it in the secret place, and no man shall know it, and the shame that shall be seen on many faces shall not be seen on your face. Therefore, in love and mercy I am instructing you, and, therefore, have I said that if a man judge himself, he shall not be judged. It is not My good pleasure that the shame of My people be seen by all. How can I judge the world if I judge not first My own house? Hearken unto these things I am telling you. If you will not hearken to Me, your shame shall be evident to all.

God's Part and Our Part

I would have you consider My life on earth—the anointing upon Me was great. Yet the temptations were great on every side, in one form and then in another, offering Me first the glory of the kingdoms of the earth, and then reviling and persecuting Me. There will be great glory given to My people, and yet the temptations shall be intensified from every side. Think not that with the glory there shall be no temptations or persecutions. The glory to My church shall be great, and so shall the temptations from the enemy to turn My people from My paths. I am warning you that when the glory shall be manifested, the temptations shall be great, until very few that start shall finish. First, there shall be offered them great worldly possessions, and then great revilings and unbelief.

Consider your Lord, that as He walked, so it shall be for you. There shall be need of great intensity of purpose. At times, everyone shall rise up against you, simply to turn you from the course that I would put you on. It is written of Me that I set My face as a flint to go the direction My Father had prescribed for Me (Isaiah 50:7). If you will finish the course the Lord has laid down for you, you

will have to set your face as a flint with great determina-
tion—you must walk in the course laid down for you.
Many of your loved ones and those who follow with you
shall persuade you and try to turn you from the course.
With many words that seem right in the natural will they
speak to you. Did not Christ rebuke Peter, who would
turn Him from the course God had prescribed? (Matthew
16:22, 23)

Understand these two things and meditate upon them
solemnly: the persecution and the darkness shall be as
great as the glory, in order to try to turn the elect and the
anointed ones from the path the Lord has laid down for
them. Many shall start, but few shall be able to finish
because of the greatness of grace that shall be needed to
be able to endure unto the end. The temptation and persecution of your Lord was continuous. He was tempted
by Satan in many forms throughout His entire life, and
even on the cross when the ungodly cried out, "If thou be
the Christ, come down from the cross." Think not that
there shall be a time of no persecution, for it shall be
from the time of your anointing unto the end—difficulties
and great persecution to the end. The Lord must prepare
you to be an overcomer in all things, that you may be
able to finish the course. The persecution shall increase,
even as the anointing shall increase.

In paths of judgment and righteousness shall the Lord
God lead His people and bring them into that place which
He has chosen for them. For the Lord has chosen a place
for His people, a place of righteousness and holiness
where He shall encamp round about them, and all who
will be led of the Lord shall be brought into this holy
place, for the Lord delights to dwell in His people and to
manifest Himself through His people. The holiness of the
Lord shall be manifested through his people. Let the Lord
lead you in difficult places. He led His people of old
through the place where no man dwelt, where no man
had passed through— in a place of great danger, and in
the shadow of death. The Lord will indeed lead His people through such places, and yet He will bring them out

into a place of great glory. Understand that the way toward the glory is fraught with great danger, and many shall fall to the right or to the left; many shall camp on lesser ground, but the Lord has a place of holiness, and no unclean things shall dwell among His people.

Put your trust in Him, and He will bring you into a place of holiness. He desires to bring His people into great glory, the like of which has never been seen: what the Lord will do for those who put their trust in Him. It is a place of darkness and great danger that separates His people into the place He would have them walk in. He will protect them from the voices that would turn them from His path. He will bring them through the dark places, and through the treacherous paths, out into the light of His glory. He will rejoice greatly over His beloved, and cause you to be filled with joy unspeakable. He seeks to lead His people into a new place of grace and glory where He will indeed encamp among them. Put your trust in Him, and He will surely bring you into this new place.

Fear not the days to come, but fear this only: that you shall walk in a manner pleasing to the Lord. In this time I am ordering and setting up My church, and it shall indeed be pure, without spot or wrinkle. I will do a work in My beloved that has not been seen since the foundation of the world. I have shown you these things that you may seek the Lord diligently with all your heart, and that you may be a preserver of His people.

Run not to this one nor to that one, for the Lord has so ordained that salvation is in Him, and in Him alone. You shall not turn to this shepherd, or to that one; for there shall be a great scattering upon the earth. Therefore, look unto Him, for He will indeed make these things clear to you. You shall not look here nor there, for wells that once had water shall be no more. But, as you diligently seek Him, He shall increase your strength and your faith that He may be able to prepare you for this time that is coming.

The truths that I have revealed to you must become a part of you, not just an experience, but a part of your very nature. Is it not written that I demand truth in the inward parts? It is the truth of the Lord expressed in your very being that shall hold you. Many shall experience the truth, but the truth must become a part of you—your very life. As men and women look upon you, they will hear not only the voice, but see the expression of the truth. Many shall be overcome because they are not constant in My ways, and because they have not permitted the truths to become part of them. I am showing you these truths that you may be prepared and having done all, to stand.

SEDUCING SPIRITS AT WORK

The Word of God warns us about the role of deception during these end times. In 1 Timothy 4:1; 2 Timothy 3:6 and 3:13, we are warned: In the last days shall come seducing spirits that shall turn many away. Many shall fall through divers lust and because of sin abounding. These "seducing spirits" try to fool God's people into trading the truth for deception. THEY TRY TO DECEIVE GOD'S PEOPLE IN AREAS THAT ARE CONTRARY TO THE WORD OF GOD. THEY TRY TO MAKE SOMETHING WRONG SEEM INNOCENT. TO PERFORM THEIR ACTS OF SEDUCTION THEY ATTEMPT TO MAKE THEIR ENTICE-MENTS IRRESISTIBLE. THEY TRY TO MAKE THE DIFFER-ENCE BETWEEN BLACK AND WHITE SEEM LIKE A SHADE OF GRAY. IF WE DO NOT KNOW THE WORD OF GOD AND DILIGENTLY SEEK RIGHTEOUSNESS, AND HATE EVERY EVIL WAY, THEN WE WILL BECOME SUSCEPTIBLE TO SEDUCING SPIRITS, FOR THIS IS ONE OF THE GREATEST DANGERS IN THE LAST DAYS.

One of the instructive aspects of Brother Frodsham's prophetic warning deals with *three great temptations* used by the Enemy during the final days to deceive or seduce God's people. The church in America is besieged in our society through the beast-system by these temptations today.

Worldly Possessions

The first of these is: "there shall be offered God's people great worldly possessions." This is a very powerful device; one that claims many victims. As Christians yield to material pursuits, their spiritual fighting skills become dull and sluggish. Those concerned only about financial success and material comforts miss the spiritual battle taking place around them. A false sense of spiritual pride develops. These Christians believe they have everything under control, but in reality, they are under Satan's influence.

American society attaches great importance to material prosperity. Many of God's people place greater emphasis on fulfilling the physical needs and wants of their families than on providing for their spiritual needs. So many of us rush here and there, making deals, hunting for bargains, doing business. We work long hours, juggle our credit lines, organize yard sales all in an effort to catch up, hold the line, or get ahead. It never ends. There's no rest for those seeking financial security. No matter how much we have, we need more. We talk and think the most about the very things Jesus told us not to worry about: what to wear, what to eat, what to drink.

Realize that Christians attachment to the things of the world is abnormal behavior. It's not just a question of paying bills and incurring additional ones. The "spirit of merchandising" has spread throughout our nation and controls the hearts of many through the power of the media. We are confronting the work of demons. The present state of people's response cannot be accounted for in any other way. Satan uses the things of the world to lure us into deception. The more we are preoccupied with the day-to-day demands of life in twentieth- century America, the less room we have for eternal concerns.

The solution to our problem is not to quit buying, selling, eating, or drinking but to learn how to avoid being led into Satan's trap. He transforms daily realities of life into major worries by altering our response and commitment to them. The cross of Christ forever shattered Christians faith in the things of this world. Paul said, "May I never boast except in the cross of our Lord Jesus Christ, through which the world has been crucified to me, and I to the world" (Galatians 6:14).

Fear of Reviling

The second temptation has to do with "the great revilings." The word "reviling" means to discredit, dishonor, berate, and ridicule. To revile someone is to attack that person's credibility. The temptation here is for Christians to idly watch the erosion of biblical standards. No one wants to be ridiculed. So Christians, because they fear the world's rejection, do not stand up against the sinfulness of the world. Because of this, the salt of America has lost its saltiness, that is, our ability to preserve that which is good. We have freed Satan to do anything he wants to so long as he doesn't threaten our own pleasures and possessions. We are apathetic about spiritual warfare, craving only the sense of security that comes from being in sound material standing.

As a nation, Americans are better off than most people around the world. It's easy to feel good about everything we have, and to credit our economic system for providing it. Many other countries have failing economies, faulty delivery systems, and chaotic social structures. We like to say that our system is superior. They have lost, we have won. But in God's eyes, we have become wretched, pitiful, poor, blind and naked (Revelation 3:14-18). Our Christianity is lukewarm.

Unbelief

The third temptation warning is "Unbelief." Christians who yield to this temptation are lulled into believing that God will not carry out His judgment against unrighteousness—that God does not really mean what He says.

Implanting thoughts of doubt culminating in outright denial of God's Word was Satan's very first attack technique. Adam and Eve had one command to obey, "not eat from the tree of the knowledge of good and evil" (Genesis 2:17). Satan tricked (beguiled) them into thinking that nothing would really happen if they ate the forbidden fruit. They disobeyed because they preferred Satan's lie to God's warning.

Unbelief has greatly weakened the Body of Christ in these last days. Unbelief is so deadly because it leads to compromise. Christians who deny that God will do what He says He will do, live carelessly. They are unafraid of God's judgment, and feel free to immerse themselves in worldly pursuits. They lose their sense of walking in holy fear of the Lord.

Worldly standards have completely captured modern thinking. Concern for others, mercy, love, and compassion have been replaced by demanding our own rights and getting our fair share. This way of thinking manifests itself in the tremendous amount of litigation in America. Americans—many Christians included— increasingly go to court to get what they want. The United States has nearly as many lawyers as the rest of the world combined. More than 650,000 men and women practice law in the United States today; that's one lawyer for every 350 people. Confidence in God has been replaced by confidence in the world system.

Mixture with the World

We must learn to fight and stand firm against any compromise within the Christian life. Those who teach and

minister righteousness must live in agreement with
God's Word. They will speak forth that which is wholly
true, and not mix with the standards of the world. Mixture is the mark of a deceiver. Deceivers speak the words
of righteousness and truth, but later, after the people
have been won over, they reveal their deceitful doctrines. Those who are asleep at the wheel are taken in;
their lives take a turn for the worse.

To better understand the treachery of compromise,
take a look at the following chart. It stands to reason that
since biblical standards never change, Christian standards should never change. But as Christians rub elbows
with the world's standards, and as Satan gradually low-
ers the world's standards, Satan wins. If we continue only
to maintain the same distance between the world's standards and Christian standards, then our Christian standards will also drift downward. The net result is that
what was a worldly standard 20 years ago, is today an
accepted Christian standard.

Biblical Standards

Media Magic

Satan has always tried to get Christians to doubt truths about God and His Word. However, his power to accomplish this has never been greater. Never in the history of the world has Satan had the means to influence the way Christians think as he does today. Present-day mass communication media affords Satan easy access to Christians inner beings. The Christian community has never had to deal with a threat of seduction like this before.

Satan's most effective use of our electronic media, of course, occurs through television and the movie theater. These devices capture both our ears and our eyes, and in the end, our minds and hearts. Poets have described the eyes as the window of the soul. The way Satan looks at it, the eyes present a channel to the heart that can be reached via television. How many think of television as a teacher? It is! Anyone—or anything— that has the ability to plant thoughts in our minds is a teacher—and a potential deceiver. People, particularly young people, are frighteningly susceptible to video images. They act out the behaviors they see modeled on the screen—including violent behaviors. Government-sponsored research has shown the impact of television on violence. In 1982, the National Institute of Mental Health (NIMH) reviewed studies done over the previous ten-year period. The NIMH report emphatically concluded that TV causes violence.[2]

TV-inspired violence is only the beginning. The endless array of "harmless" programs—the "decent" movies, game shows, and commercials communicate the ungodly message of self-centeredness. Television offers "entertainment" which overdevelops the sense of self. Personal sacrifice, delayed gratification, and giving to others are alien themes. Television promotes the desires of our sinful nature, the lust of the eyes, the lust of the flesh, and the pride of life. It teaches people to look out for themselves and their own interests. Christians learn to trust in their own resources rather than look to the Real Source.

The creation of electronic media in the twentieth century has allowed Satan to capture the human imagination as never before in human history. The expansion of cable and network television in recent years has provided Satan with a medium of influence for every minute of every hour of every day. A curious invention of the 1920s, TV rapidly became part of American households after World War II. Before the '50s, television (and radio) stopped broadcasting at ten o'clock in the evening. But in 1950, late-night television began to appear. Since then, the idea that there should be time and space reserved for private family life has vanished. Today, the stream of films, programs, and commercials pour into American households around the clock. Tolerance, and eventually indifference, to sin results from being exposed to, and falling under the seduction of electronic teaching media.

It's impossible to overstate the impact of video on modern society. Did you know that the United States leads the world in the production of TV programming? The American film and television industry has no significant foreign competitors. Total U.S. television program exports are estimated to be about 150,000 hours; 50,000 are sent to Latin America, 50,000 to Asia, and 50,000 to Europe. Programs such as "Gunsmoke," "Bonanza," "Star Trek," and "Dallas" have been viewed in far-away places like Japan, Israel, and Norway. We export our immoral lifestyle across the globe; we influence the people of other nations adversely. America's economic prestige is slipping, but American cinema has never been greater. America's—the beast's—power of worldly influence is beyond imagination.

UNDERTAKING SPIRITUAL WARFARE

Given the prevalence of seducing spirits today, it's important to know how to resist them. There is a spiritual truth in Scripture that is seldom discussed today, yet if we are to walk in spiritual victory over the influence of the seducing spirits, it is vital that we understand it.

The Sinful Nature

Mankind's sinful nature is not removed when a person becomes a Christian. It's important to understand this. Those who have accepted Christ into their hearts have not lost their will to sin. The sinful nature—the flesh—is still there; it's part of every believer's inner make-up. Experience tells us this is true. What happens at the point of conversion is that the person makes contact with a power source greater than the sinful nature. This power source is the Holy Spirit, that is, God Himself, who is a Spirit.

> Yet to all who received him, to those who believed in his name [speaking of Jesus], he gave the right [or power] to become children of God—children born not of natural descent, nor of human decision or a husband's will, but born of God. (John 1:12-13; see also Acts 2:38–39)

We cannot see the Holy Spirit. We can only see the way He affects people. People begin to be victorious over sin after they are reborn spiritually, and oftentimes their personalities change.

We become the temples of the Holy Spirit of God when we are reborn spiritually (1 Corinthians 3:16). The Spirit enables us to obey God's Word and live a holy life. He motivates righteous living. However, we can only experience victory over our sinful nature to the degree that we allow the Holy Spirit to control our thoughts and actions. That is why it is so important for us to learn not to quench the Spirit (Ephesians 4:30).

When we quench God's Spirit, our old sinful nature takes charge of our thoughts and actions. This produces selfish actions, even while doing "Christian" activities. Tempers flare, jealousy begins, pride develops. The quest for position, power, and recognition takes priority when Christians quench the Spirit of God, preventing His control over our inner nature. When we yield to the world's thoughts and accept its standards, we stop the flow of God's power. Losing contact with God's power spells defeat for the Christian and the cause of Christ. James writes:

> Who is wise and understanding among you? Let him show it by his good life, by deeds done in the humility that comes from wisdom. But if you harbor bitter envy and selfish ambition in your hearts, do not boast about it or deny the truth. Such "wisdom" does not come down from heaven but is earthly, unspiritual, of the devil. For where you have envy and selfish ambition, there you find disorder and every evil practice.
>
> But the wisdom that comes from heaven is first of all pure; then peace loving, considerate, submissive, full of mercy and good fruit, impartial and sincere. Peacemakers who sow in peace raise a harvest of righteousness. (James 3:13-18)

We need to be firmly established in God's Word. If we trust in the personalities of men, we will be moved by the seducing spirits. We are to follow the path of righteousness and diligently inquire of the Lord when we hear of something that we have not seen in the Word. When we place our admiration for a person above God's truth, seducing spirits unfold their deception.

The Struggle Within

Everyone who becomes a Christian, a true believer, becomes a battleground. The struggle for control of the believer's thoughts and actions takes place continually. The Holy Spirit of God gives us a new nature (we are His creation—born anew) and empowers us to walk right-eously. Satan wages war against our new nature by constantly tempting us through our old sinful nature and the seducing spirits of his world system. We must be constantly alert and self-controlled if we are going to walk in victory over sin, because the Devil goes about like a roaring lion, seeking someone to devour (1 Peter 5:8).

The apostle Paul discovered this inner spiritual warfare. He described it by saying that even though in his mind he wanted to keep God's law, he found there was another law at work in his being. It was the law of sin. The "law of sin" is an inner force leading Christians to do things they know they should not and keeps them from doing those things they know they should. Only after Paul learned to "walk in the power of God's Spirit" did he gain victory over the power of his sinful nature (see Romans 7:18 through 8:17).

Satan is well aware that we are slaves to the law of sin. Therefore, we need to be aware that Satan's objective is to keep us from walking in the power of the Holy Spirit— that supernatural power God equips us with to overcome the sinful nature. Many Christians today do not seem to be aware of the fact that we are engaged in such a terrific spiritual battle. Consequently, they casually expose themselves to the temptations of Satan's seducing spirits as part of their daily lives. (More about the law of sin in Chapter 9.)

Denying the Power

God has equipped us for spiritual warfare. We can resist the temptations of modern life. Paul writes:

> No temptation has seized you except what is common to man. And God is faithful; he will not let you be tempted beyond what you can bear. But when you are tempted, he will also provide a way out so that you can stand up under it. (1 Corinthians 10:13)

The Lord promises to deliver us if we seek Him. He will give us the victory if we acknowledge our reliance on him.

But this is not going to be easy. In 2 Timothy 3:1-5, Paul forewarns that living the victorious Christian life in the last days will be very hard. Many will deny the power of the Holy Spirit and be taken prisoner by seducing spirits. Paul says this will be evident by the characteristics expressed through God's people. He writes to Timothy:

> But mark this: There will be terrible times in the last days. People will be lovers of themselves [the cause, I believe, for so many of our personal conflicts], lovers of money [the focus for many of our Christian activities], boastful, proud, abusive, disobedient to their parents, ungrateful, unholy [immoral], without love, unforgiving, slanderous, without self-control, brutal, not lovers of the good, treacherous, rash, conceited, lovers of pleasure rather than lovers of God — having a form of godliness but denying its power. Have nothing to do with them. (2 Timothy 3:1-5)

These same self-serving anti-Christ characteristics which have become so dominant in our society will control our lifestyle if we are not controlled by the indwelling power of the Holy Spirit.

In Chapter 3 of 2 Timothy, Paul teaches that in the end times many will possess the Christian label. Many call themselves Christians and display a form of Christianity, but are not truly devoted to God. These individuals have been overcome by seducing spirits; they are deceived and so they put out the Spirit's fire. Paul instructs devoted Christians to have nothing to do with those people (2 Timothy 3:5). Basically, he is telling us not to listen to self-loving, self-seeking, self-serving "Christian" teaching. He emphasizes Christians need to be filled with the Spirit in order to dampen the power of our self-centered, inner, sinful nature. This is even more critical in these last days with the ability of the beast-system to reach our inner nature through the media. Certainly this is one of the reasons why he declared it was going to be difficult to lead a committed Christian life in these last days.

The proof is in the heart. Those empowered by the Spirit always seek to do what is right. This was true in the life of Jesus, the apostles, and many Christians throughout the centuries. God's Word has not changed.

> Lord, who may dwell in your sanctuary? Who may live on your holy hill? He whose walk is blameless and who does what is righteous, who speaks the truth from his heart and has no slander on his tongue, who does his neighbor no wrong and casts no slur on his fellowman, who despises a vile man but honors those who fear the Lord, who keeps his oath even when it hurts, who lends his money without usury and does not accept a bribe against the innocent. He who does these things will never be shaken. (Psalm 15)

THE FRUIT OF DECEPTION

American Christians are fulfilling the prophecy spoken by the Apostle John. Using the beast-system as his primary weapon, Satan is waging war against the church. Seducing spirits have sapped Christians strength and have trampled over them in their weakened state. It's not that it's impossible for believers to experience victory in their lives today, but that so many of them have lost sight of what it means to live victoriously. The seducing spirits Paul tells Timothy will appear in the last days and that Brother Stanley Frodsham warned about, have erased Christians ability to discern right from wrong. Too many Christians have been influenced away from the path of righteousness by Satan's deceptive devices.

It is impossible to measure the extent to which worldly standards have clouded man's receptivity to Christian teaching. But we know it has had disastrous consequences. Concern for others takes a back seat to the pursuit of more and better things. Dependence on God has been replaced by confidence in modern day technology. The self-centered lifestyle that rules our society has produced epidemic levels of crime, violence, drug abuse, homosexual freedom, the AIDS plague, child abuse, broken families, corrupt business practices, and blasphemy against God. See Paul's list in 2 Timothy 3:1-5. There is no denying the fact that seducing spirits at work through the beast-system have produced widespread spiritual heart disease within the American people.

Chapter 5

SPIRITUAL HEART DISEASE

As seducing spirits spread the seeds of deception throughout American society, Americans are reaping a bitter harvest of suffering and defeat. Satan has undermined our families, our public schools, our government, our way of thinking, and our social order. Violence, immorality, and disease have taken a heavy toll on the American people. So many people experience hurt and pain, and many Christians do not know why. It's sad to think about the moral deterioration of our society and the tragedy it causes, but do not despair. We must recognize the problem before we can find the solution.

This chapter concentrates on the essence of the problem—the heart. Satan is winning the battle for control over the hearts of American Christians. He knows where we are most vulnerable. Jeremiah 17:9 states: "The heart is deceitful above all things." It's because so many Christians do not have their hearts right with God that this nation is on the decline. To find the reason behind the corruption and chaos we need look no further than ourselves.

HEARTS OF DARKNESS

Cardiac arrest, or "heart attack," is the leading cause
of death in the United States. According to the American
Heart Association, more than one million Americans suffer a heart attack every year. Millions more suffer from
strokes, high blood pressure, or related conditions.
Nearly half of all deaths in this country each year result
from cardiovascular disease. Over 60 million Americans
have one or more forms of heart or blood vessel disease.
Cancer runs a distant second place as a cause of death.
Every minute of every day, three Americans have heart
attacks.

The poor physical condition of the American people's
hearts is unquestionable. Heart disease is quite possibly
the worst plague the world has ever known. It certainly
has devastated the United States. The American Heart
Association estimates that in 1988, cardiovascular disease cost $83.7 billion when the expenses of physician
and nursing services, hospital and nursing home care,
medications, and lost productivity are tallied. Yet many
people throughout the world are not plagued with heart
disease. Death from an acute episode of heart disease is
virtually unknown in many countries.

Has it ever occurred to you that the condition of Americans' physical hearts may be God's way of telling us
about the condition of our spiritual hearts? Could there
be a spiritual parallel between these two conditions?
Personally, I had not considered the connection until the
Lord gave me a vision of the spiritual heart condition of
the American Christian.

The Vision

Picture yourself standing outside a door. You walk up
to the door and turn the knob but the door is difficult to
open. The door barely opens a few inches despite the

exertion of steady pressure. You realize that something on the other side is blocking the door. So you put your shoulder to the door to force it open; it gives another inch or two but that is all. Something on the other side—some powerful binding resistance refuses to allow the door to open. It is impossible to open the door because of a heavy assortment of items stacked against it: clothes, toys, furniture, and other household goods. All of these items are piled up behind the door—between it and the wall of the room you are trying to enter—they stand between you and an open doorway and prevent your entrance. It soon becomes apparent that no one can enter the doorway until all of the things in the way are removed.

During the spring of 1990, while I was sitting in church during the song service, a vivid picture of this doorway appeared in my mind. I could see Jesus standing outside the door. He was trying to open the door but it would scarcely open a few inches. In the picture in my mind, I could see exactly why the door would not open; there were so many things piled up behind the door—between it and the wall—that He simply could not get in. The Lord was knocking, leaning, and pushing but the resistance was too strong. He was trying to open the door but the space it would open was too narrow for Him to enter.

I could recall only one other time I had a vision like this one, so it certainly got my attention. (Although I use the word "vision" to refer to what I saw, I do not know that it is the only word that should be used to describe it—there may be a more appropriate word.) The picture of Jesus standing at the doorway was so clear, so distinct, yet unrelated to my train of thought at the moment that I knew it was given by the Spirit of God. I knew it had spiritual significance. During the next hour and a half of that worship service, I sought the Lord for understanding. As the service came to a close, I began to accept that such understanding would not come at that time. I had prayed and asked God to help me understand the vision because I thought its meaning was possibly something I needed to share with the congregation.

Then as quickly as the picture of Jesus standing in the doorway had earlier leaped into my mind, my spirit was quickened with a revelation of its meaning, and I understood the vision. The Lord Jesus was standing at the door to the hearts of Christians here in America. He was there knocking, even pushing at times, at the door of our hearts wanting to completely enter and become Lord of our lives. I could see that He not only desired to open the door to our hearts, but He was trying to enter and fill our hearts. But our hearts' door would barely open. The door would only open wide enough for Him to catch a glimpse of what was inside, and so He was able to occupy only a small portion of our hearts. Christians in America let Him control very little of their lives.

Next, the Spirit of the Lord revealed the meaning of all the things behind the door that were preventing Him from opening it. All of the things blocking the doorway represented our attachments to the world. Just as the tremendous heap of clutter kept Jesus from opening the door in my vision, there are so many worldly things piled up in our hearts and they keep the Lord from entering fully and ruling completely. The Spirit also revealed that what makes up this barrier of things from the world varies from person to person. The worldly attachments that prevent the Lord from taking over one person's life might be quite different from the things kept in the way by another person. Finally, the Spirit showed me that the worldly barricade symbolized the spiritual state of most Christians in America.

The meaning of the vision had come to me just as the service ended. Although it seemed a bit unusual for me to speak at the end of the service, I knew the Lord wanted me to walk up front, share the vision, and interpret its meaning. So I did.

Physical Heart Disease

The vision I had that Sunday morning led me to see a link between physical and spiritual heart disease. It also led me to do some research about heart disease. In order to better understand the spiritual lesson, it is necessary to have some basic knowledge of physical heart disease.

Arteriosclerosis is the technical term for hardening of the arteries. Medically speaking, it refers to the infiltration of fats within artery walls which causes the accumulation of plaque in the circulatory system. As more and more plaque develops, increased clogging of blood arteries occurs. And as plaque accumulates, arteries narrow. Consequently, the flow of blood to the body's vital organs is restricted. Too much plaque may result in the stoppage of blood flow, or it may result in a blood clot. If a clot occurs in one of the coronary arteries—the channels that supply the heart with life-sustaining blood—a heart attack results.

Plaque is the reason for all the recent concern about the consumption of saturated fats and cholesterol. Too much saturated fat in the diet and too much cholesterol in the bloodstream promotes an excessive amount of plaque. The accumulation of plaque within the arteries is one of the most dangerous, unhealthy (often deadly) things that happen to the human body.

You may think my comments about plaque are motivated by a desire to promote natural foods. It is true that some of the processed foods available on grocery store shelves and those foods sold at fast-food restaurants contain unhealthy amounts of saturated fats and cholesterol. Medical professionals agree that the consumption of high-fat, high-cholesterol processed foods is one of the main reasons that heart disease has reached epidemic proportions in the United States compared to other nations. But I am less concerned about the benefits of natural foods than the spiritual parallel between wide-spread heart disease in America and Americans clogged relationship with God. It is only because my spirit is burdened by the vision I believe the Lord gave me that I am writing about heart disease.

To review: plaque accumulates on the walls of arteries, the build-up of plaque hardens and narrows arteries, and hardened arteries lead to the restricted flow of blood, blood clots, heart attacks, and death.

Things of the World

Just as I defined some of the terms used with physical heart disease, I will discuss those terms associated with spiritual heart disease. In my vision it was revealed that spiritual plaque is a build-up of "things of the world" in our hearts. Contrary to what many believe, this phrase does not necessarily refer to material possessions. In Scripture, the word "world" has three primary meanings. First, it refers to the material universe (including the earth) as in Matthew 13:35. Second, world refers to the inhabitants of the earth, or mankind, as in John 3:16. Third, world is used to mean the moral and spiritual systems which bond humans together otherwise known as "human society."[1]

Society is that realm of the world developed by the efforts of man. It consists of man-made religions; political structures and governments; economic, business, and financial systems; educational systems; science and technology; along with entertainments and amusements. Eliminate these things and you eliminate society; they make up what is meant by the phrase "things of the world." These are the things of the world John refers to when he says: "Do not love the world or anything in the world. If anyone loves the world, the love of the Father is not in him" (1 John 2:15). (Other verses contain the same principle, including James 1:27, James 4:4, and Ephesians 2:1-2.) The key word is "love" which means committed or attached to any worldly thing.

Since the fall of Adam and Eve, society has been made up of systems developed by man. Unless converted, mankind is trapped in an unregenerate or lost state spiritually. A person is not a member of God's family or under God's inspiration as long as that person is not converted and freed from Satan's control (see Ephesians 2:1-2). In other words, all of the things produced by mankind in an unregenerate condition fall under the influence of Satan. Unless God intervenes for some special reason, humans are only capable of developing the things which make up human society or what John calls the "things of the world." Society is that part of the world developed by mankind rather than created by God. To love or be attached to any of the things produced by society (which includes commitment to religious organizations and beliefs not given by God) is to give the Enemy ammunition to attack one's spiritual commitment to Jesus as the Lord of life.

This is not to say that the things developed by mankind cannot be removed from the world system and claimed for the glory of God. Just as the inhabitants of the world can be converted, so can the things they construct. But the point is that Christians need to acknowledge God's warning about the things of the world and Satan's control over them, and they need to be alert as to how the Enemy uses them to wage war against their commitment to Jesus.

According to Scripture, the whole structure of our society is ordered by a principle of life that is foreign to God and leads people away from Him. Satan uses the material world, the people of the world, and the value systems of the world against God's people. Satan has perfected his use of worldly things to such an extent that they have greater power today than they have had at any other time in world history. No longer does worldly contact depend on going out into the world. The staggering advancement of electronic technology and communication networks today enables the world system to find Christians wherever they are. It captivates people daily. Christian families must be alert to the pull and power of the forces of evil in the world as never before.

Most Christians recognize that they have been under the bondage of sin. They readily agree that sinful things emanate from Satan, but far fewer Christians agree that many things in society are under the control of Satan. Most of us are still of two minds about this. Yet Scriptures clearly affirm that "the whole world [human society] is under the control of the evil one [Satan]" (1 John 5:19).[2]

Satan knows very well that to try to influence and deceive Christians through activities they clearly recognize as sinful is vain and futile. The Bible does not teach that this is his method. Satan is too smart for that! The Christian community will usually flee from the things they identify as dangerous. Instead, Satan has fabricated an enticing worldly society—the beast-system—in which he artfully weaves the things of the world around people to entrap unsuspecting Christians. This is how he gets Christians to commit adultery with the world.

We need to understand the tactics Satan uses to attack Christians and stop the flow of our spiritual blood—the life of Jesus in our hearts. In the field of international relations, government officials realize that national survival depends on knowing foreign enemies. In business and sports, it is essential to know the competition. In medicine, doctors and other medical professionals know the great danger that heart disease has become. Certainly Christians dedication to the spiritual realm must be even more crucial than these human endeavors.

When God's people fail to recognize and combat Satan's schemes, spiritual heart disease deepens.

We who make up the American church live carelessly and flirt dangerously with darkness. Before we can expose sin in the world we must see our own sinful lives.

> For you were once in darkness, but now you are light in the Lord. Live as children of light (for the fruit of the light consists in all goodness, righteousness and truth) and find out what pleases the Lord. Have nothing to do with the fruitless deeds of darkness, but rather expose them. For it is shameful even to mention what the disobedient do in secret...Be very careful, then, how you live—not as unwise but as wise, making the most of every opportunity, because the days are evil. (Ephesians 5:8-12, 15-16)

Just as plaque is the dangerous villain in our bodies, the things of the world endanger our spiritual life. It was the things of the world heaped up behind the door in my vision that kept the door from opening wide enough for the Lord to enter. Our spiritual strength varies in direct proportion to the extent we allow the life-sustaining life of Christ to fill our spiritual heart. The characteristics of Christ are revealed in our lives only through His life within us.

The way the modern food industry processes the food eaten by so many Americans is a major factor for plaque accumulation and heart disease. In the same way, the world system is responsible for a diseased spiritual life. Our materialistic society constantly tempts us to seek pleasure and weighs us down with anxiety and pressure which lead to commitment to the things of the world. Jesus warned this condition would develop in the last days. He said, "Be careful, or your hearts will be weighed down with dissipation [excessive pleasure], drunkenness and the anxieties of life" (Luke 21:34). I think most Christians would admit that the things of the world impinge on their spiritual lives. The worldly pressure which leads Christians to attach themselves to the things of the world often becomes greater than their commitment to obey the Word of God.

HYPOCRISY VS. SINCERITY

In the physical realm, the blockage of blood flowing through our arteries causes blood clots, strokes, heart attacks, and other complications. In the spiritual realm, the blockage of the life of Christ flowing through us causes many spiritual complications. One of the worst spiritual heart diseases we can have is a dishonest, insincere, deceived, or hypocritical heart. All of these adjectives describe a common heart disease: believing we are more mature spiritually when we are not. Hypocrisy is a lie with an attractive cover in which the inner working of the heart does not match outer behavior (see Matthew 23).

Hypocrisy

The heart disease of hypocrisy has been the worst of all spiritual heart conditions throughout the history of mankind. Hypocrisy opens the door of our hearts to deception which blinds us spiritually. Deception caused Adam and Eve to fall. It caused wickedness to become so terrible across the earth that God had to wash it with a cleansing flood. Deception allowed Satan to develop the spirit of rebellion and permissiveness so strong in God's chosen people—Israel—that Israel often turned against the ways of God. The Israelites were unable to recognize their Messiah, Jesus when He came. Deception caused the church in Europe during the Dark Ages to become so blind that God had to prepare a place of near obscurity to protect the true church and His Word.

The opposite of a sincere heart willing to reveal sin is a hypocritical heart which tries to hide sin. It is extremely difficult to persuade a hypocrite to uncover lusts and openly confess sins before God. Just as sincerity of heart and confession of sin results in God's faithfulness to forgive and cleanse (1 John 1:9), hypocrisy brings contempt of the heart before God. God speaks harshly about hypocrisy because He hates it so much. "Nevertheless they did flatter him [God] with their mouth, and they lied unto him with their tongues. For their heart was not right with him" (Psalm 78:36-37 KJV). Woe to the man who dishonors God in the name of honoring Him!

God often pays the hypocrite—whether a person, a people, or a nation—a portion of the wages of sin in this life. Ananias and Sapphira died by the hand of God with a lie on their lips. Peter asked Ananias, "How is it that Satan has so filled your heart that you have lied to the Holy Spirit? ... You have not lied to men but to God" (Acts 5:3-4). Even if the hypocrite crosses over to eternity before the mask is removed, the hypocrite will face God's anger. It will be of no comfort to realize then that so many others, including himself or herself, had been fooled. Hypocrisy of the heart is the loudest lie of all because it is heard directly by God Himself. Jesus reserved his most scathing denunciations for the religionists and hypocrites of His day. The Psalmist says "Blessed is the man ... in whose spirit there is no deceit" (Psalm 32:2 RSV).

The abomination of hypocrisy also lies in the fact that it walks around in spiritual robes and boasts a personal relationship with God. Hypocrisy claims to share in Christ and His righteousness, and in the consolations of the Spirit. These are spiritual crimes which bear a heavy penalty. Essentially, any portion of a hypocritical heart within our being mocks God. The same is true of formality in religious service. The hypocrite often appears to outdo the committed Christian, yet God looks at the heart, and He knows better. Judas confidently sat down with the apostles at the Passover as if he were the most welcome, holiest guest of all, yet his heart was evil and he betrayed Christ.

No one will be faster than the hypocrite to claim the grace and comfort of the Holy Spirit. This is evident in the actions of the Pharisees who desired to have a holy name. "Verily, I say unto you," Christ said, "They have their reward" (Matthew 6:2 KJV). Many profess to believe in God but deny Him by their actions. They speak boldly of their kinship with Christ, but the actions of their lives are far from heaven.

Hypocrites, playing out their religious roles, may even bring about some apparent good by giving a measure of comfort to the sincere. But that is when the sincere are in most danger because they do not suspect misdoing. Religion seems to be the most effective bait of hypocrites to ensnare others in their ways. Hypocrites try to lure and seduce others into participating in a lifestyle that is in conflict with the Word of God. This relieves them of guilt and massages their troubled consciences. Do not sample the free gifts and give-away graces of stage-playing saints. Keep a measured distance to avoid being lulled by seducing spirits into error.

Hypocrites often speak the truth first to cover their sins. Christians are to be firmly planted in God's Word, not the sayings and personalities of men. We are to keep ourselves holy and walk in paths of righteousness before the Lord. Only then will our eyes be opened and will we be protected by the Lord.

Hypocrisy rooms next door to insincerity. Many expressions of outward Christian zeal find hypocrisy at base. It requires wisdom and grace not to allow hypocrisy to reside in our hearts. Satan and his diabolical instruments muddied Job's life, but Job's spirit continued to flow from an honest heart before God. Our Lord will change our hearts if we are willing to have them changed. Be careful not to make a false profession of your spiritual state. Claiming to be one place spiritually and actually being another place is a great deception. It is the desire for holiness, pure love, and unfeigned faith that proves soundness of heart and brings forth evidence of Christ in our lives.

David's Sincerity of Heart

David is called a "man after God's own heart" because he carried the image and desire of God's heart within his spirit. God's Word was engraved upon his heart so that there was no guile or compromise. Because of David's honesty and sincerity, a sense of life radiated from his being; it was a gleaming mark of honor which awarded him the honor of carrying the name of God. David counseled his son Solomon to "serve him [God] with wholehearted devotion and with a willing mind, for the Lord searches every heart, and understands every motive behind the thoughts" (1 Chronicles 28:9). It is the sincere heart that is ready for spiritual responsibility because that heart is merged with God's will. Even when our best effort fails, willingness of heart means success to God.

David was the anointed servant of the Lord when the results of his sin became evident. The key part of the sequence is the reaction of his heart. He did not try to excuse or hide his sin when his spiritual eyes were opened and he saw what he had done. He knew he had done wrong and was ready for God's judgment. Likewise, the sincere Christian pleads for mercy before God and waits to hear what He has to say. We must submit ourselves to be searched by having our conscience exposed and our hearts opened. We no longer seek self-pity, but learn to walk with our heart's door open wide. Our spiritual journey may be interrupted, but just as soon as the trouble ends, we return to the walk of holiness because this is our new nature. "Blessed are they who maintain justice, who constantly do what is right" (Psalm 106:3).

God desires to create in us a pure, honest, and sincere heart void of hypocrisy. Sincerity of heart keeps our soul's credit at the throne of grace. A sincere heart will support even a weak hand to turn the key in prayer. The gospel covenant relaxes the rigor of the law and speaks in terms of sincerity and truth in our hearts. A sincere heart is the Christian seeking Christ's interest, not personal interest. God accepts the person whose heart is right with His heart. God exalted Caleb to a towering place because of his uprightness: "But because my servant Caleb has a different spirit and follows me wholeheartedly, I will bring him into the land he went to, and his descendants will inherit it" (Numbers 14:24). Caleb's sincerity of heart brought him honor before God.

The sincere heart is a simple, elegant structure; the old heart is a crowded, complicated construction. The pure heart is like a mountain stream: clear, plain, and clean. The pure heart continually searches for remnants of the old and avoids excuses or the temptation to smooth over problems. That God might be justified is the aggressive thrust of the changed heart; it desires to root out all sin and develop the heart characteristics given by Jesus. "Search me, O God, and know my heart; test me, and know my anxious thoughts. See if there is any offensive way in me, and lead me in the way everlasting" (Psalm 139:23-24). When confronted with irrefutable evidence, the sincere heart, absent of all hypocrisy, pronounces judgment upon itself. Just as David confessed, the sincere heart confesses, "I have sinned against the Lord" (2 Samuel 12:13).

A Lesson From Israel

Throughout history, God's people have had trouble recognizing and accepting their true spiritual state. The prophet Malachi informed the people of Israel that God would destroy what they had built in their wickedness.

They refused to believe God's message of judgment was for them (read the book of Malachi). Similarly, God spoke to the Israelites through Isaiah:

> Shout it aloud, do not hold back. Raise your voice like a trumpet. Declare to my people their rebellion and to the house of Jacob their sins. For day after day they seek me out; they seem eager to know my ways, as if they were a nation that does what is right and has not forsaken the commands of its God. They ask me for just decisions and seem eager for God to come near them. 'Why have we fasted,' they say, 'and you have not seen it? Why have we humbled ourselves, and you have not noticed?' Yet on the day of your fasting, you do as you please ... Is that what you call a fast, a day acceptable to the Lord? Is not this the kind of fasting I have chosen: to loose the chains of injustice and untie the cords of the yoke, to set the oppressed free and break every yoke? Is it not to share your food with the hungry and to provide the poor wanderer with shelter — when you see the naked, to clothe him, and not to turn away from your own flesh and blood? (Isaiah 58:1-3,5-7)

If you continue to read Isaiah chapter 58, you will find that God makes many promises to those who live in righteousness.

More recent history reveals that God's people have repeated the same mistakes made by the Israelites. The Jews established a tradition of interpretation which denied inner commitment and made keeping God's laws purely an external matter. Not only had the prophets warned them, but when Jesus came, He called attention to the error of this hollow interpretation by Jewish leaders. Jesus told them what God intended. He explained clearly that God looks at the heart, not merely outward performance. But since most Jewish leaders developed from their own human wisdom the idea of what God was like, Satan was able to deceive them with religious independence and spiritual pride so they were blinded. They could not recognize God when He came to them in the flesh in the person of Jesus Christ.

We should learn this lesson well because the Jewish leaders knew the Scriptures and honored the name of God yet they were still deceived. They were zealous in their desire to serve God but their eagerness was according to man's wisdom. They were unwilling to sacrifice themselves to the spirit of the law, nor to the *Lordship* and *character* of God to direct their lives. Like the Jews, Christians today often reject the total, surrendered life because of indifference to spiritual needs. We are too busy with worldly activities and pursuits and are caught up in the treadmill of daily existence. Our inner spiritual being has become secondary. Like them, we know the Scriptures intellectually and honor God's name. We want to serve, but we want to serve by human wisdom and willpower. The true Spirit of Christ and His glory is lost in our involvement because our hearts are really seeking to satisfy our selfish lives.

This condition exists because Christians do not know how to rid themselves of the spiritual plaque caused by things of the world. Too many of us are not even sure that to remove ourselves from an attachment to worldly things is necessary. Our society controls our minds because most of us remain under the continuous influence of the media (radio, television, films, magazines), educational philosophy, and the lure of material success. The spirit of self centeredness across our land has brainwashed us. This continual bombardment of worldly ways is identified by John as "the lust of the flesh and the lust of the eyes and the pride of life" (1 John 2:16 KJV). Worldly influence has become so powerful, so intense that most of us can barely keep from clinging to some of the self-seeking ways of the world system in which we live. This last-days deceitful attack on Christians is prophesied in the Bible. Many times we cannot see its effect on true spiritual commitment. The Bible says that it will even deceive the elect without God's intervention (see Matthew 24:24).

THE TRUE HEART

The greatest teachings on spiritual heart commitment are found in the words of Jesus. In the greatest sermon ever preached, the Sermon on the Mount found in Matthew 5-7, Jesus focused on the heart. Here Jesus described the inner heart characteristics of the committed Christian. These heart characteristics are a mirror for us to examine ourselves, not a window through which we look at others. Jesus' teachings on the heart call for unrestricted, relentless, complete investigation; they are quite different from the worldly religious teachings. The Beatitudes express what the Christian's heart should be like.

Heart Characteristic #1: Poor in Spirit (Matthew 5:3)

"Poor in spirit" means empty of self-interest. This heart characteristic is the key to everything that follows in the development of the Christian walk. It deals with the process of emptying us of our old sin nature so we can be filled with the power of God's nature, His Holy Spirit. Satan's character is self-centered, and the selfish characteristic in each of us must go the way of the cross to be made inactive. Notice how Jesus' teaching directly conflicts with all that is of this world. We tend to look at other people and their personalities, intelligence, business success, natural abilities, personal appearance—all the worldly characteristics. We even promote these characteristics in church. However, none of these characteristics draw people to Jesus. They draw people to other people and personalities.

Isaiah described Jesus as someone so unattractive that no one would be naturally drawn to Him (Isaiah 53:2-3).

Only Jesus' quality of humility withstands trials and storms. The world system despises the quality of poor in spirit. Satan uses all the tools available in our world society to promote the self-centered ways of the flesh.

Heart Characteristic #2: Mourning (Matthew 5:4)

The characteristic of mourning is to see sin in ourselves and in the world. Recognizing sin as sin is an attitude Satan wants us to avoid. Satan tries to develop in us a desire to escape from reality; the desire to avoid seeing sin for what it is. The major theme of worldly pleasure—including money and the energy and enthusiasm expended in the entertainment world—is an expression of Satan's goal of moving us away from the spirit of mourning.

Mourning allows us to experience deep inner pain over the sin of the world. We need to see our natural, sinful self and recognize the principle of sin at war within our inner being. Jesus mourned when he saw sin in the world. He saw its terrible result of pain, sickness, grief, despair, and death. He saw sin sending masses of people to hell and eternal damnation. This is why sin should bring mourning; mourning is the state of seeing what sin does to people and how it stabs God in the heart. The degree to which we possess this characteristic plays heavily in the appreciation we have of God's deep love, our Christianity, and our commitment.

Heart Characteristic #3: Meekness (Matthew 5:5)

Meekness is that heart characteristic which centers on our relationship to others. Jesus brings us face to face with the nature of man when he describes the characteristic of meekness. We naturally rely on the strength and power of our personal abilities, intellect, and aggressiveness to influence the world. Yet Jesus says, "the meek shall inherit the earth" (Matthew 5:5). Jesus' teaching on meekness baffles the wisdom of man in the world. Meekness does not mean flabby, weak, shiftless, or ambitionless. A meek person is not easy going, "nice," spineless, or willing to compromise to achieve peace at any price. Examine how Jesus lived. His life demonstrates that meekness does not mean weakness.

Meekness was the lifestyle of Jesus, Moses, David, Abraham, Peter, Paul, and many others throughout the history of God's people. These meek followers of God became servants to others regardless of the personal cost. They did not rely on their own abilities or take the things God wanted them to accomplish into their own hands, but submitted their self-wills to God and became totally dependent on Him. Meekness is to have a true view of oneself.

Moses was one of the greatest leaders of all time and Scripture describes him as a meek man (Numbers 12:3). He was to be head of all Egyptian civilization, and through the authority of this position, surely he could have accomplished the Israelites return to Palestine. But God purged Moses of his self-power, position, and abilities and allowed his mission to be accomplished only by His character and His power. It was not by worldly power which is man's way, but by the Spirit of the Lord, which is God's way (Zechariah 4:6).

The same was true of Jesus. He took the form of a man and became a servant. He did not use the political systems of the world to accomplish God's mission. Instead, He sacrificed himself and gave His all for others. His meekness confounded worldly ways, but meekness is the way that works. Examine its eternal results.

It is the heart quality of meekness which causes us not to demand anything for ourselves. When people

scorn, slander, or berate us, meekness means that we
will not lash back in retaliation. Meekness means no
longer being concerned about self, promoting personal
interests, or defending personal rights. Meekness means
never demanding position, privileges, possessions, or
status in life; never being defensive about ourselves,
our opinions, or the rightness of our position. Self-life
has gone to the cross; it has been crucified. Meekness
allows us to truly see ourselves and our inner state and
to realize that our former state was not worth defending. To possess this characteristic is to no longer be
sensitive about ourselves; we are now vessels for God
to live in and through.

Heart Characteristic #4: Hunger and Thirst for Righteousness (Matthew 5:6)

As the Christian develops the first three heart characteristics discussed, we can see the Lord's perfect
sequence for being emptied of self—our old nature. To
the degree that we are emptied of our self-seeking
nature, we will desire to be filled with God's righteousness. The Lord will turn that desire into hunger
and thirst. Righteousness provides genuine peace. It is
the Christian characteristic that shows a definite sign
of our Christianity. It was His righteous nature which
distinguished Jesus from all other men.

To hunger and thirst is to be aware, to be conscious
of a deep and desperate need, to the point where we
have deep, soulful pain. This sense of need remains
until satisfied. This kind of hunger and thirst is like the
inner drive an athlete must possess to become a cham-
pion. The drive is so desperate it hurts. It is an all-out
commitment to sacrifice.

It is important to note that Jesus did not instruct us to
hunger and thirst after happiness or blessings. Happiness and God's blessings are the result of seeking after

righteousness. Seeking after them is to make the same mistake as a doctor who treats the results of disease rather than the cause of disease. Jesus directs us to live for righteousness because only righteousness can fill a person emptied of self.

You can see why Satan uses all of the many elements of the world system to deceive us and prevent us from self-emptying—dying to self-interest and the things of the world—this blocks our spiritual arteries. Not dying to self-interest eliminates our inner hungering and thirsting for righteousness. It also hinders our being filled with God's spiritual power. If one is emptied of the self-seeking nature and filled with God's nature, the next three heart characteristics describe the new nature that controls one's personality and behavior.

Heart Characteristic #5: Merciful (Matthew 5:7)

To be merciful means to have pity, compassion, and sorrow and to act on these sentiments. Mercy is the heart characteristic that allows us to see others through a different eye, a Christ-like eye. Our attitude toward others changes when we begin to see people as creatures to be pitied, creatures that are slaves of sin, creatures trapped within Satan's deceitful world, creatures bound for hell as we once were, creatures that need forgiveness as we need forgiveness.

Mercy distinguishes between the sin and the sinner. Because Jesus was merciful, He was moved to say "Father, forgive them for they know not what they do." Jesus could see that those who persecuted Him were actually victims of Satan's world system. Because God is merciful, He took pity on mankind and made salvation available through the sacrifice of His Son as atonement for our sins.

Heart Characteristic #6: Pure in Heart
(Matthew 5:8)

Purity of heart is single-minded devotion to God. It is a heart devoid of self-interest. Having a right heart is the very foundation of the Christian doctrine. When Jesus bypassed the intellectual mechanics of Scripture and zeroed in on the heart, he baffled the scholars of His day. He made it clear that Christianity requires a change from the inside out. It requires a whole new heart.

Through this heart characteristic Jesus identifies the seat of all our problems. It is from the heart, Jesus teaches, that evil thoughts, lies, blasphemies, and immorality proceed (Matthew 15:19). A heart problem is the source of every life problem; every unworthy desire comes from the heart. To allow the Lord to develop in us a new heart brings freedom from hypocrisy. Only with a new heart will we have the singleness of mind needed to truly know, glorify, love, and serve God. A pure heart seeks God's will in nature, in historical events, and in our own lives.

Heart Characteristic #7: Peacemaker
(Matthew 5:9)

Peacemaking is one of the cherished qualities of all Christian characteristics; it is the one all Christians should cry out to God to burn into our lives. We should desire Him to change our lives through the other heart characteristics so that we can reach spiritual maturity. Only then can the quality of peacemaking become reality. Of all the aspirations in the history of mankind, inner peace is the chief goal humans strive to possess. It is God's greatest desire that His children be the vessels that bring peace on earth and goodwill to men.

Being a peacemaker does not mean being an easy-going person who wants peace at any price. A peacemaker is not a person who keeps quiet just to avoid trouble or a person who appeases others all the time. A peacemaker has been delivered from self. Meekness allows the peacemaker to be absolutely neutral when surrounded by conflict, to be totally free from defensiveness and hypersensitivity. The peacemaker's interest is focused on bringing inner peace to mankind regardless of personal sacrifice. The peacemaker sees a larger, more important purpose for life than protecting personal rights. The supreme example of a peacemaker is Jesus. He sacrificed His rights and went to the cross to provide the hope of peace in our hearts.

Like Jesus, the peacemaker's primary concern is the glorification of God among His people. The peacemaker views all disputes, whether between individuals or nations, as distractions which detract from the glory of God. The peacemaker is selfless, loving, and approachable; when other people sense a peacemaker, they approach knowing that they will receive understanding and direction which will lead to peace in their hearts. People are drawn to Jesus because He is a peacemaker.

The blessing promised to peacemakers is a tribute to all Christians. Jesus says that "They will be called the sons of God." In essence, Jesus is saying "Like father, like son," for when a Christian displays peacemaking, Jesus says "This is truly being like a son of God."

Persecuted for Righteousness (Matthew 5:10)

Being persecuted for the sake of righteousness is not an inner quality of the heart, but an outer characteristic of the Christian life. The Christian who has the inner heart characteristics just described will be persecuted verbally and possibly physically.

People persecuted Jesus because His nature was so different. His righteousness, which exposed the righteousness of those around Him as insincere, superficial, tasteless, and vain, also dredged up the evil darkness of those who refused to believe they were evil. His light was so bright it had to be extinguished, so the forces of darkness persecuted and killed Him. Other righteous Christians throughout the history of the church have generated similar resistance; the characteristics of their hearts provoked a hateful response from those people around them who could not accept the power of the Christians inner light.

The spiritual heart characteristics of a Christian are contrary to the wisdom and ways of the natural man. The natural man considers them foolish although they are the true secret of happiness. In His sermon, Jesus said that "blessed", in other words "happy", are those who have these qualities of heart. These heart characteristics reveal what a Christian professes. They show us that *being* is more important than *doing*; actions or works should result from being. The characteristics of the Christian heart are meant to control us, not for us to control our Christianity. As Paul says:

> I have been crucified with Christ and I no longer live, but Christ lives in me. The life I live in the body, I live by faith in the son of God, who loved me and gave himself for me. (Galatians 2:20)

As members of God's family, the heart characteristics Jesus described should become our new nature. The new nature must come about through the power of the indwelling Holy Spirit; it is impossible for the new nature to come about by self-will. Even the most brief examination of the heart according to these spiritual heart characteristics reveals that it is impossible to achieve them through personal will. The new nature is completely opposite of the world and the way worldly people naturally function.

Although a careful look at God's true character is often crushingly painful, it helps us to realize that only complete dependence on God will enable us to live a Christian life in a world that is directly opposed to the characteristics of that life. Most of today's technology Satan uses to keep hearts closed to the truths of these heart characteristics Jesus gave in the Sermon on the Mount.

The only way these heart characteristics can develop is for our heart's door to open and allow the fullness of Christ to enter. In my vision, the Lord revealed that most Christians in America are deceived and remain attached to the things of the world. This attachment acts like spiritual plaque in that it keeps the door to their hearts blocked. We need the fullness of Jesus in our hearts now more than any other time I can think of considering the power our society has to expose us to its worldly ways. We need to be freed from the worldly power of society which influences our thinking and controls the characters of our hearts.

THE AMERICAN HEART CONDITION

Today, as we near the time of our Lord's return, we can be sure that Satan has launched an all-out attack. We have a serious problem of spiritual heart disease in our country. We can choose to be deceived and say that things are great spiritually because we would like them to be that way. But if we are honest and do not trust feelings or desires, I believe we must admit that the fruit reveals rottenness.

The spiritual war for America is at a turning point. If Christians do not begin to fight, to learn how to stand firm, and to live according to God's standards, then the Christian heritage established at America's founding will lose its influence altogether. Christian standards are already blending with those of the world. The true meaning of commitment to God's Word and His standards of righteousness is fading into the past.

I am greatly concerned about the spiritual deterioration of our society, and I am not alone. Many spiritual leaders today point out that America is under a heavy spiritual attack. David Wilkerson, James Dobson, Bill Gothard, Bill Bright, Pat Robertson, Billy Graham, Chuck Colson and others have spread the message that Christians need to get serious about their relationship with God. From what I can see, these men are burdened for our country, and they have committed themselves to organizations devoted to ministry. It's important to listen to what they have to say. It reflects the severity of the American people's spiritual heart condition.

Satan's Attack on the Family

The Christian family is under siege. The age-old tradition of motherhood has come under such heavy fire recently that one researcher who examined ten sets of textbooks used in elementary schools throughout the country found there was hardly a story that celebrated motherhood as a practical, meaningful way of life:

> Ruffling through the pages of your daughter's school books what you won't find is a single image celebrating the work women do as wives and mothers. That information has been carefully and systematically purged from the official cultural record. Our society is making young mothers victims of a pre-programmed guilt trip.

Perhaps Theodore "Teddy" Roosevelt said it best when he stated that "if the mother does not do her duty, there will be either no next generation, or a next generation that is worse than none at all." She teaches, ministers, loves, and develops character. She challenges her children to do their best; she nurtures precious lives given by God. Yet the editorials do not value these accomplishments, nor does our culture give the coverage mothers deserve. This is just another of the many areas we have allowed the liberal movement of the 1960s and 1970s to win in the battle of spiritual warfare.

Dr. James Dobson, Founder and President of Focus on the Family, and Gary L. Bauer, President of the Family Research Council (and who served as President Reagan's Domestic Policy Advisor) recently, wrote a book titled *Children at Risk*.[3] This book details the battle in our society for the hearts and minds of our kids. Every parent and grandparent needs this kind of information and more. Speaking about our culture, they write:

> The same twisted philosophy that permits us to kill infants through abortion with impunity is now prevalent throughout the western world. This new way of thinking has produced a society that is extremely dangerous to minds and bodies of children.
>
> At the arrival of adolescence, teenagers are subject to the pressure and wrath of their peers, making them prime targets for brainwashing. The mind-bending process at which television and movies constantly hammer away at moral values and principles. Any form of self-discipline or restraint is usually ridiculed by friends and acquaintances. This develops a lot of pressure for conformity, until finally, many of our youth trade in their freedom for slavery and domination. Their behavior has been warped by the enormous social pressures coming through society. This opens the doors of temptation which carry many names: alcohol, marijuana, hard drugs, pornography, gambling, homosexual experimentation, premarital sex and more.
>
> It should be clear that one of our jobs as parents must be to keep these temptation doors closed, locked and barred to adolescents. It is frightening today to see that these doors are not only unlocked for many of our youth—they are wide open. It is no wonder that the kids who want to remain chaste are often made to feel like prudes and freaks.
>
> With the heartache and illness the loose humanistic standards are now causing for the families of our society, one

would think responsible adults would be united in a campaign in opposition. But normally the contrary is found to be true.

Dr. Dobson, in his book, points out some of the inevitable results of eliminating restraints. Human-centered value systems have come to dominate our thinking; they have scorched our land, spreading like wildfire with disastrous consequences. Some thirty-eight sexually transmitted diseases are spreading in epidemic proportions. Sellers of pornography, worldly music, immoral television programs and movies profit from the youthful passions and the irresponsibility of our young. The government spends billions to assist children and families yet suicide is one of the top killers of young people. Drug abuse is rampant. The frequency of sexual assaults on children is staggering. Child abuse occurs daily as millions of cases are reported annually.

Poison in the Public Schools

Public schools in this nation face an even greater problem than faltering academic standards. They deserve a failing grade when it comes to instilling morals. The moral poverty of public education becomes painfully obvious with even a brief look at school discipline, or should I say, the lack of discipline. According to Gospel Films, the top seven discipline problems in public schools in 1940 and 1983 were as follows:

1940	1983
1. Talking in Class	1. Rape
2. Chewing Gum	2. Robbery
3. Making Noise	3. Assault
4. Running in the Halls	4. Burglary
5. Cutting in Line	5. Arson
6. Improper Clothing	6. Bombing
7. Littering	7. Murder

Since 1983, the situation has worsened. Drug use and abuse is widespread. Teenage pregnancies have reached record highs in many school districts. Condoms are now freely distributed in New York City public schools without parental consent. Guns and other weapons turn up in lockers. Yet teachers are no longer allowed to pray, nor are Christian students allowed to discuss the subject of the Lord in many schools. Textbooks and teachers preach secular humanism in nearly every academic subject. Is it any wonder our schools erupt with decadence and violence?

Humanistic thinking has captured public education. Secular humanists know if they can control what young people are taught— what they see, hear, think and believe—that they can determine our nation's philosophical outlook for generations to come. That is why they take every opportunity to ridicule this nation's Christian heritage and Bible-believing Christian standards. Consider this disturbing fact. By 1989, three-fourths of public school students had sex education. Public school teachers are duty-bound to teach sexuality from a humanistic philosophy, and this has had dire consequences. Out-of-wedlock pregnancies among high school students have increased, not decreased. Twelve-year-olds discuss oral sex and the most intimate adult subjects. Seventy percent of high school seniors report to having had sex. It's almost as if virginity has become a rumor and pre-marital sex the norm.

Public school officials not only condone premarital sex play in the hallways, but have selected a text advocating it in some schools. *Boys and Sex,* by Wardell B. Pomeroy, is a "how to" book filled with detailed information for male sexual conquest. No wonder "date rape" is now running rampant in high schools and colleges. Research at 35 universities revealed that 25 percent of the female students have been victims of rape or attempted rape. Ninety percent of them did not tell police, which means that the actual amount of rape is even higher.

Virtually every known perversion has been presented in sex education classes and most parents are in the dark because they never have had an opportunity to examine the curriculum. School officials have called for volunteers to teach youngsters how to use condoms. Who do you think volunteers? Militant homosexual groups such as ACT-UP! Homosexuality has become an open and "valid" lifestyle. The *Wall Street Journal* recently ran a front-page feature about homosexuals demanding and obtaining the right to teach their lifestyle in some public high school sex education classes.

There are certainly Christian teachers in our public schools (12 percent of public educators profess Christianity), and I am thankful for them because they are so desperately needed. However, the Christian minority will tell you that the majority are not Christians. The poisonous textbooks used in the classrooms and the immoral conduct allowed in the hallways in public schools today are an abomination to the Lord.

Not only are schools morally bankrupt, they are failing to teach the three R's. After 26 years of teaching in New York's public schools, John Gatto won the "Teacher of the Year Award." Instead of praising the system that honored him, he openly criticized the system when he went to Washington, D.C. to accept his award. In an interview with the *Washington Times,* Gatto said: "As my kids performed better, I attracted hostility from the school establishment, which surprised me. I was genuinely intrigued." That fall (1991), he refused to go back to the system. He traveled around the country on a crusade for "alternative schools" and "free-market choices."

The philosophy of high school graduates today reveals that many have been educated contrary to traditional values. This is evident by their lack of respect for religion, and at the same time, their commitment to humanistic values. If young people are to learn integrity, self-control, honesty, and respect for authority, it will have to be taught somewhere other than the public school system.

Government Under the Influence

The light of our Christian heritage has burned brightly for many generations — until the current generation that is. Why has it been extinguished so quickly? I believe it is because we are seeing come true what Abraham Lincoln said: the philosophy of the classroom today will be the philosophy of the government tomorrow. It may be convenient to believe that Americans still live as "one nation under God," but the truth is, government bureaucrats in our "anything goes" society have criminalized religious speech in many aspects of public life. Christian symbols in public places are immediately attacked with the full authority of the government. Students who pray in high schools are silenced. Crosses atop public buildings during Christian holidays are torn down. College students brave enough to oppose the homosexual rights agenda on their campuses are criticized for intolerance and labelled "homophobics."

What does it say about the moral fiber of our nation when the President openly recognizes the homosexual lifestyle? Mr. Bush distinguished himself as the first president ever to do so, when he honored several homosexual activists by inviting them to the White House for the signing of the Hate Crime Statistics Act of 1990. The President's invitation to homosexual activists to join him at our nation's capital did not signify his personal approval of the homosexual lifestyle. However, his action inadvertently granted respectability to an immoral lifestyle with a corrosive influence on our society. Chuck Colson,

Founder and Chairman of Prison Fellowship, aptly said of this incident: "The President made a poor—and dangerous—decision."

In the meantime, Christians cannot exercise their right to non-violently protest against abortion clinics. The abortionist's knife claims over one and a half million lives each year. Or, what about the federal officials who expect you and I to subsidize art (so-called) "that portrays Christ as a heroin-shooting drug addict"—and— "depicts the cross of Jesus in a jar of urine"? Yet this same government prohibits prayer at the beginning of a school day, forbids displaying a nativity scene in a public park, outlaws placing a cross on public land. In 1989, the Supreme Court in which witnesses must still swear on the Bible to tell the truth declared a nativity scene at a Pittsburgh courthouse unconstitutional. Christians have allowed the cultural elite to sweep away in one generation what millions of Americans formally embraced as desirable values. Something is radically wrong here.

M. G. "Pat" Robertson, President of the Christian Broadcasting Network, stated in his 1990 November-December perspective:

> The clear message from the recent elections is that the voters in the United States have no real interest in correcting the nation's precipitous fiscal and moral decline.
>
> Voters returned to office a U. S. senator who wanted to establish a tax-funded department for New Age paranormals, and who brought psychic spoon-bender Uri Geller to a key arms control meeting. They reelected a homosexual congressman whose homosexual aide runs a call boy prostitution business from the congressman's house. They seemingly ignored the Savings and Loan bailout imposed on the taxpayers. Except in two instances, no congressman was defeated who voted to raise taxes to fund blasphemous and pornographic art.
>
> No congressman or senator was defeated because of the ill-considered last minute budget nightmare, the on-

going huge budget deficit, higher taxes, or congressional pay raises. The United States economy is standing closer to a 1929 style depression than at any time in the past 60 years.

The eligible voters had a chance to make a change. They refused to act decisively. Therefore, they have ratified the snowballing moral and financial decline which has been destroying the nation. Ninety-eight percent of all members of the House of Representatives were reelected.

As time goes on you will see that it will be our government that promotes the "new world order." It will be the superpower behind the realignment of nations.

Crime and Violence Everywhere

Violent crime in the United States occurs with greater frequency than in any other nation in the world. *The Arizona Republic* daily newspaper ran a cover story on March 19, 1991, entitled: "Nation Engulfed by Crime." This article showed that a violent crime wave unmatched in the 214 year history of our nation has arrived. For example:

> In 1990, Americans killed, raped, robbed and assaulted each other in record numbers, about 6 million incidents … The average citizen runs a higher risk of becoming a violent crime victim than of being involved in an automobile accident. More teenage males, black and white, die of gunshots than from all natural causes combined. In the past 30 years, the level of violent crime has grown 12 times faster than the population.

We no longer can hide our faces from the fact that there are reportedly 100,000 gang members in the state of California alone. Since the "sexual revolution," hundreds of thousands of morally-sick people prey on our children. Hundreds of child pornography magazines are distributed daily throughout our land; these are purchased by individuals who fantasize about sexual acts with young boys and girls. Regardless of what homosexuals would like for us to believe about their lifestyle, it commonly involves "auto cruising" or some other method of searching for young, fresh sexual partners. No wonder parents must keep a fearful close eye on their children while out shopping or at the ballgame.

David Wilkerson wrote in his October 15, 1990 message that episodes of random, pointless violence are no longer confined to the inner-city. Where can a person go to escape from the demonic spirit of violence that rages in this country?

> For instance, about three years ago a family of five left New York City and settled in a quaint little village upstate. They thought they were safe from the crime and violence of the city. For two years their home seemed like paradise to them. But recently the father, mother and two of the children were found dead in their country home, each shot in the head by an unknown intruder!
>
> Even in the mountains of Colorado, once a pleasant getaway, devil worshippers rape and plunder. Animal sacrifices abound. Now we've even been warned that it is unsafe to camp in every one of our great national parks. A lawless, violent wave has been vomited out of hell, not only in the major cities, but even into the smallest towns across America, and inside the gates of limited access communities!

In our major cities, the new wave of valuelessness has left crime and disorder in its wake. It is impossible to properly describe the horror many people have experienced. For example, in 1952, New York City had 5,757 robberies. In 1989, it had 93,387—a stick-up every 6 minutes. Girls were raped and thrown off roof tops; one boy was tied-up, then set afire. The murder rate is headed toward six per day. Recently, in one 24-hour period there were 17 murders plus numerous other violent, but nonfatal attacks. The Big Apple has 500,000 drug abusers. The illegitimacy rate in central Harlem is eighty percent and rising. Each year 10,000 babies are born "toxic"— addicted to cocaine. Each of these will cost $220,000 for medical attention before they reach kindergarten. Los Angeles is also a city on the verge of exploding. Drug gangs—white, black, Hispanic—fire weapons at innocent passersby. They have no morals, no conscience. They kill only for the enjoyment.

Not only does the reality of violent crime threaten our neighborhoods and our families, imaginary violent crime has become a popular form of entertainment. So many TV programs, movies, and paperbacks are dedicated to criminal violence that recreating criminal acts has replaced baseball as the national pastime. Americans love to watch and read about people being assaulted, robbed, raped, and murdered. How else can that be explained except to say that Americans simply cater to their sinful natures? We celebrate violence as no other society, exporting our violence-ridden popular culture to the detriment of other countries throughout the world.

GOD'S NEXT MOVE

The spirit of worldliness that has invaded our society is bound to be hard to accept. No one likes to hear "doom and gloom." It is depressing to think about everything that's wrong with our society. But it's necessary to accurately gauge America's spiritual state in order to prepare for God's next move. I do not believe that peace and prosperity waits around the corner, that this nation will rebound with a few minor adjustments. I believe that God will judge America for its wickedness. God did not spare his chosen people, the Israelites, and he will not spare uncommitted Christians.

Chapter 6

GOD'S COMING JUDGMENT

The subject of judgment, or discipline, is certainly not a popular topic even among Bible-believing Christians. It is, however, one of the most important truths in the Bible. Judgment is God's way of correcting those He loves, whether it be a person, a people, or a nation. "Whom the Lord loves he chastens" (Hebrews 12:6). God disciplines His people when they become misguided and careless. He brings judgment when they allow deception to take root in their hearts and grow to control their minds.

We usually think of judgment as something negative, but when administered by a loving judge, judgment produces something good. Discipline, when carried out properly, is one of the greatest acts of love. Proper discipline requires a loving disciplinarian who acts despite personal feelings. A loving disciplinarian places the overall well-being of the one in need of correction above the inner hurt and pain experienced by carrying out the discipline. Uncompromising discipline and sacrificial love go hand in hand.

Several men of God declare that America is racing toward judgment. Pat Robertson writes that God's judgment is imminent.

We must recognize that in Europe, America, and parts of Asia, the rebellion against God continues to crescendo. Murder, rape, looting, family breakdown, sexual permissiveness, militant homosexuality, blasphemous films and music, the widespread embrace of satanism and the occult, unbelievable wasteful and luxurious living by the rich, and open denial of God and Christian values by the western establishment—the educators, the philosophers, parts of the church, the media, the film community, and government leaders—have opened our society to the very real possibility of devastating judgment by a Holy God. The question is no longer *will* God's judgment fall on the earth, but *when*.[1]

Romans chapter one teaches that when homosexuality can openly be proclaimed in a society, it is a sign God has given that nation up for judgment. In this chapter, I will share what the Lord has revealed to me on His coming judgment. Before I do that, I want to discuss America's spiritual inheritance, review some scriptural teaching about accountability and responsibility, and consider the American church's spiritual condition.

AMERICA'S SPIRITUAL HERITAGE

Our nation has been abundantly blessed in many ways. America has benefited from God's blessing over and above most nations throughout history. This is especially true from a spiritual perspective. Even a brief look at our nation's past reveals how God watched over and provided for the spiritual development of America. The founding of our nation was a new event in the history of humanity. As the Constitution reveals, our nation was founded on scriptural principles. Central ideas in the Constitution can be traced to powerful biblical preaching which took place during the Great Spiritual Awakening in the 1700s.

God continually raised up anointed men like John Wesley, George Whitefield, Charles Finney, and Dwight L. Moody to shape the development of our country. Especially when one considers the founding of America, the significance of God's miraculous hand in America's spiritual development cannot be denied.

Our country witnessed a new beginning in the life of the church. Today, churches that profess to teach and preach the Christian message can be found every few blocks in most towns all across the nation. Over 250,000! Bible teaching can be heard day and night on radio and television. The Bible remains the nation's number one bestseller and millions of books with a Christian message are sold each year. American missionary organizations spend millions of dollars to preach the gospel throughout the world. Funds are also available in America to translate, print, and distribute the Word of God. Christian elementary schools, high schools, and colleges make Christ-centered education possible for the nation's young people. There are numerous other Christian organizations, outreaches, and activities as well.

Undoubtedly, God has graciously blessed America with a tremendous Christian heritage. Christianity has been the dominant religious faith in America from the beginning, and Americans benefit from that influence today. Americans have complete freedom to know, to worship, and to be committed to serve Jesus Christ, God's son and our Savior.

PRIVILEGE MEANS ACCOUNTABILITY

We are accountable for the resources and opportunities God has given us. Accountability in our relationship with God is a scriptural principle. "From everyone who has been given much, much will be demanded; and from the one who has been entrusted with much, much more will be asked" (Luke 12:48b). God's principle of accountability and obedience can be found throughout the Old Testament in His relationship with the Israelites (see Deuteronomy chapter 28 for example), and in the New Testament, particularly in the letters of Paul and other apostles to the churches. Clearly, our relationship with God cannot be a one-way street.

We often hear about the benefits of being in God's family— the inner peace and the promise of heaven and eternity with God— but we do not hear as often the message that we Christians are accountable for our lives in this world. We should know, however, that living a righteous life is not optional. We cannot focus solely on the benefits. The Bible commands us to be holy because God is holy (1 Peter 1:13-16). We are to be a people full of good works who humbly reach out to those in need or who have problems. As members of God's family on earth, we are to be the salt (the preservers of good), and a light set on a hill (pure in heart, striving to avoid sin, not accepting worldly standards).

The fruits produced by the present generation indicate that the church, the Body of Christ, has ignored God's principle of accountability. Our lives no longer testify that we are a saved people, holy, set apart in the family of God to proclaim His righteousness. We do not want to be held accountable for living such an obedient life style. We have listened to the call of the world and adopted its slogans which tell everyone to be independent and do their own thing. "Be your own person!" the world says. We have become victims of prevailing spirits, characterized by an indifference to sin. "No accountability!" we say. We want to be left alone to pursue our own interests. We don't seek direction, or even want to hear about true commitment that requires sacrifice on our

part. God has given us such a rich Christian heritage plus
the freedom to live out our faith, but the evidence
reveals that we are not keeping its purity.

RESPONSIBILITY INCLUDES POWER

Just as we are accountable for our Christian inheritance and obedience, we are responsible for resisting the
enemy and standing for the righteous standards of God.
God has equipped us to fulfill this responsibility in our
Christian life every day— at home, at work, at play, wherever. "Finally, be strong in the Lord and in His mighty
power," the Bible says, "put on the full armor of God so
that you can take your stand against the devil's
schemes...so that when the day of evil comes, you may
be able to stand your ground" (Ephesians 6:10-13). The
day of evil is here, yet we are not fulfilling our responsibility to stand for righteousness.

We need to realize that there is no middle ground in the
area of spiritual warfare. There is only right versus wrong,
good versus evil, light versus darkness. We will either
stand our ground or lose ground, conquer or be conquered, tread on or be tread upon, stand or fall. Riding-
the-fence is not possible; we are counted among the
forces on one side or the other. The battle line has been
drawn by Satan who "prowls around like a roaring lion
looking for someone to devour." The Bible commands us
to "resist him, stand firm in the faith" (see 1 Peter 5:8-9).

We must also realize that the advantage is ours. We have
been given both the power and the authority through
Jesus Christ to stand, resist the enemy, and win the battles
for God's righteousness. Consider these Scriptures:

> The one who is in you [the Holy Spirit] is greater than the
> one who is in the world [Satan]. (1 John 4:4)
> In all these things we are more than conquerors
> through Him who loved us. (Romans 8:37)

No temptation has seized you except what is common to man. And God is faithful; he will not let you be tempted beyond what you can bear. But when you are tempted, he will also provide a way out so that you can stand up under it. (1 Corinthians 10:13)

But beware! If we are spiritually lazy, soft, or lukewarm and do not rely on the spiritual authority God has given us to resist and fight battles, God will relinquish the power and authority to our Enemy. In spiritual warfare, without God's power, Satan will overcome us. In this last generation, Christians have been overcome in many areas. John predicted this when he prophesied about the beast-system. "It [the beast-system] was allowed to make war on the saints [Christians] and to conquer [overcome] them" (Revelation 13:7). God allows Satan to test our faithfulness and challenge our commitment to His righteousness. This is evident in the testing of Job, the temptation of Christ, and the history of God's people.

Many things in the spiritual realm are difficult to comprehend, which is one reason we must learn to live by faith. One principle should be clear, however. When we claim a position of spiritual authority (which we are to do as members of God's army), we can expect that authority to be contested and challenged. Authority must be contested by the opposition because it is the only way it can be tested.

If we fail to use the power and authority God has given us, we can expect terrible consequences. A severe penalty follows spiritual ineptitude, one that brings shame, humiliation, and disgrace upon the church. Lack of spiritual commitment to the standards of God's righteousness cannot be hidden from God or from the world for very long. To be sure, our sin will find us out. In this last generation, Satan and his world system have challenged our spiritual walk as never before.

"Who can rightly define and establish God's righteous-ness?" you may ask. Mankind has debated this issue since Adam and Eve ate the fruit from the tree of knowl-edge of good and evil (Genesis 2:15-16; and chapter 3). The natural man has always attempted to establish and work out his own standards of right and wrong, good and evil, justice and injustice, and then strives to live by them.

As Christians, however, we are different. Since we were converted—became members of God's family—a new sense of righteousness has developed in us. The result is that we, too, are occupied with the question of good and evil. But it is important for us to realize that for us, the starting point is a different one. We do not begin from the matter of man's ethical right and wrong. We do not start from the tree of the knowledge of good and evil.

Jesus Christ is the Tree of Life. We begin from Him! He is our standard of righteousness. The principle of con-duct that establishes our code of righteousness is the principle of the cross and the indwelling life of Jesus Christ. His Sermon on the Mount sets forth an overview of His standards of righteousness and the principles that should govern our Christian walk (Matthew 5 through 7). His focus is on the heart—the spiritual part of our being—not only the outward appearance the Pharisees emphasized. If the Christian's heart is right before God, his or her outward appearance and actions will be right also.

THE POWERLESSNESS OF THE CHURCH

Is the American church (God's people) full of right-eousness? Walking in the Spirit? Overcoming sin? Does the Christian church live in glorious victory over the power of mankind's inner self-centered nature? Are we a people with clean hands and pure hearts who have their affections set on things above? Or are we instead: covetous, divorcing, depressed, worldly-minded, self-loving, money-loving, compassionless, rebellious, greedy, competitive, conceited, boastful, proud, ungrateful, unforgiving, lacking self-control, lukewarm, permissive, pleasure-loving, adulterous, immoral, lustful, slanderous, abusive, and disobedient? Are we the people of the church during the last days that Paul describes (using adjectives similar to the ones I've used above) in 1 Timothy 3:1-5 who have a form of godliness, but deny its power? Read these verses.

I believe we fit Paul's description. We are unwilling to sacrifice our self-interested life style. We are failing to preserve our spiritual heritage or live by God's standards. In this last generation, we have opened the door to the Enemy and he has flooded our homes with his ways. We have invited evil into our homes. The worldly filth and garbage Christians allow to come into their homes through modern-day electronic media demonstrate this fact. The whole moral structure of our society is collapsing all around us. The Enemy is winning! With our strong Christian heritage and knowledge of God's Word, we are without excuse. The Christian church, which includes pastors and teachers, do little about the moral decay of our country. We have become part of the problem.

If God's army (that's us) had accepted the orders to do battle, the Enemy could not have produced the evil that's in America today. In this last generation, we have allowed Satan to generate crime and violence, murder millions of babies through abortion, flaunt and promote homosexuality, create an epidemic of drunkenness and drugs, and tear down our families. We have permitted Satan to produce pornography, child molestations, filthy movies in theaters and on television, and other harmful areas which erode the moral structure of our society.

Satanic fruits dominate our news every day, yet most Christians sit idly by and watch, paralyzed by advancing apathy and ignorance of spiritual principles. Our hearts are so calloused we don't even mourn as our nation becomes more and more evil and sinks deeper and deeper into sin. Whether we like to hear it or not, *we need to recognize that one of the greatest signs of our spiritual weakness and lack of spiritual commitment in the church is revealed by the sin the people of the world feel free to commit.* The fact that so many Americans *live openly* in sin reflects the condition of spiritual immaturity and weakness on the part of the American church. There is no other way to explain how the American people, living in the world's geographic center of Christian teaching, have become the world's most immoral people.

Brothers and sisters in the Lord, we have allowed our country to deteriorate spiritually to the point that God has only one option. To save us from spiritual self-destruction, He must judge our nation and discipline its people. There are too many Christian people in our country whom God loves for Him to allow our nation to continue in the direction chosen by this last generation. We have drawn a line and dared God to cross it. When Satanic powers are made welcome in any nation, it will become a habitation of demons. It must end in a living hell on earth, a devil's playground. God will not continue to allow His name, His authority, and His power to be squandered. "Those whom I love I rebuke and discipline" says the Lord (Revelation 3:19).

God is about to do a new thing in America. He is reaching the end of the line. God is going to make ready the Bride of Christ in America. Today, the bride is an adulterous bride. She has mixed with the world. We are guilty of the sin of mixture! Through God's refining and purification process, Satan and the world will come to know who has the real power. The coming judgment of the Lord will cause the Body of Christ to depend on Jesus once again, commit to walking in righteousness, and be pure in heart. The self (the "god") we now worship with our self-seeking, self-serving, self-satisfying life-styles will be consumed by God's refining fire.

We have left God no alternative but to judge the church in our land. We possess a knowledge of His ways; therefore, we are without excuse. As the Hebrew writer informs us, "if we deliberately keep on sinning after we have received the knowledge of the truth, no sacrifice for sins is left, but only a fearful expectation of judgment..." (Hebrews 10:26). As a result of the spiritual heart disease in our nation, we have reached that point where bypass spiritual surgery has become necessary to remove the worldly plague that clogs our spiritual arteries.

THE JUDGMENT TO COME

I am going to share a personal experience that previews through Scripture God's coming judgment of America. In 1988, I was awakened very early in the morning by the Spirit of the Lord. I got up immediately. I sensed that I was to go out to our family room and pray, and as I began to pray, a heavy anointing from the Lord fell on me. The anointing was so heavy that I got up from where I'd been praying and started to walk through the house, praying and crying out loud to the Lord. I can't remember everything that I prayed and cried out to the Lord about except that much of it focused on what has happened to the morality of our country, how unconcerned most people are, and the way so many people have suffered as a result.

I had been praying for about an hour when the Spirit of the Lord led me to reach for my Bible and turn to the book of Isaiah. The Lord directed me to read several chapters in a strange way. He guided me to read them in a different sequential order than they appear in the Bible. I marked each chapter in my Bible to record the sequence.

Early in the morning of January 9, 1989, the Lord spoke a divine word to my inner being again, saying that He had shown me what will happen in the future. Immediately, my spirit quickened and I knew that the Lord was referring to those chapters in Isaiah that He had given me about a year earlier.

I believe I am to share these portions of Scripture from Isaiah in the same sequence that the Lord gave them to me. I was only slightly familiar with these Scriptures before the Spirit of the Lord directed me to read them. I was guided by the Spirit to read chapter five of Isaiah first. Then, chapter three through the first verse of chapter four, followed by chapter one from the second verse to the end of the chapter. Next, I was directed to read chapter two of Isaiah beginning with verse six through the end of the chapter. Finally, I read chapter two, verses one through five, combined with chapter four, verses two through six. Here are the portions I read in order:

(1)   Isaiah 5:1-30
(2)   Isaiah 3:1-26, and 4:1
(3)   Isaiah 1:2-31
(4)   Isaiah 2:6-22
(5)   Isaiah 2:1-5, then 4:2-6

I am sure you will want to read these Scriptures on your own and seek the Lord so that He may speak to you. So, they are reprinted here with my own comments to clarify what I believe the Lord was saying to me through these verses.

The first chapter, Isaiah five, begins with a beautiful parable about God's tender care for His people and their unworthy returns for His goodness. Then in verse eight, the allegorical language ends and Isaiah reproves the people for their wickedness, particularly for their covetousness and inattention to God's warning. The prophet follows with an enumeration of judgments as the necessary consequence of their indifference.

> I [Isaiah] will sing for the one I love [God] a song about his vineyard: My loved one [God] had a vineyard on a fertile hillside. He dug it up and cleared it of stones and planted it with the choicest vines. (Isaiah 5:1-2a)

The vineyard represents God's people. They were provided with everything needed to continually produce good fruit. Isaiah is talking here about Israel's settlement in the rich, fertile land of Palestine, which was made possible by God. But we know that God's principles in dealing with man never change. The times, places, and circumstances may differ, but God is the same yesterday, today, and forever. I find the resemblance between some of the experiences of the Israelites and those of Christians throughout church history extremely interesting.

Abraham's descendants, God's earthly family, were oppressed in Egypt for several hundred years. Then God led them out to a land "flowing with milk and honey" where they were free to worship, serve, and follow God's guidance. Similarly, the history of Christianity also includes several hundred years of extreme oppression during the Dark Ages, the Crusades, and the Inquisition. Then in 1517, Martin Luther made a break for Christian freedom and the Reformation began in Europe. By 1700, the major thrust of restoring biblical Christianity and liberating God's people moved across the Atlantic to a fertile, new land called America. God kept this land from exploration by Europeans, it seems, until after the Reformation. America, too, became a land of milk and honey where God's people were free to worship, serve, and follow Him. It truly became a new and different light in the church's history.

The church experienced its own mini-exodus by moving to a new land when God began to work among the English Puritans. The Puritans faced oppression at the hands of King Charles I (1625-1649). For 16 years beginning in 1628, over 20,000 Puritans immigrated to America. The Puritans, above all others, established a Christian foundation for the new nation.

> He [God] built a watchtower in it and cut out a winepress as well. Then he [God] looked for a crop of good grapes, but it yielded only bad fruit. (Isaiah 5:2b)

The building of a watchtower symbolizes how God watched over the Israelites as they settled in the land He had given them. The same is true of God's guiding hand in the founding of America—the many great men of God, our Constitution, the Great Awakening, and the Christian institutions so important to the beginning of our nation. When Isaiah speaks of the winepress, he is speaking allegorically of God's placement of the Holy Spirit. Israel was given power to produce good grapes, which is righteousness. "It yielded only bad fruit," as Isaiah calls it, referring to spiritual weakness among God's people, that is, a general lack of commitment and powerlessness to combat sin in their personal lives and communities. I think Isaiah was probably not referring to everyone, but rather the overall spiritual status of Israel. It is the same in contemporary America, generally speaking. So many evils pollute our land, it's becoming more and more grotesque, yet Christians seem powerless to stop the desolation.

> Now you dwellers in Jerusalem and men of Judah, judge between me and my vineyard. What more could have been done for my vineyard than I have done for it? When I [God] looked for good grapes, why did it yield only bad? (Isaiah 5:3-4)

The word "Jerusalem" in these passages has a wider meaning than the actual city of Jerusalem. It identifies the center of God's spiritual life and activities at the time. The temple, the focal point of God's activity among the Israelites, was located in Jerusalem. Today, the word "church" has similar meaning to the way Jerusalem is used in these verses. The word "Judah" in this portion of Scripture has a special meaning as well. Judah refers to the nation in which God's spiritual activities take place. In Bible times, the nation of Israel was the center of God's activities. In the modern world, it has been America.

In verse four, God asks His people what more could He have given them than He had already provided to produce good fruit. He inquires about the grapes in His vineyard, which represent the standards of life that ruled the country, and finds them to be bad for the most part. The same might be asked of America today: What more could God have done for the church than He already has? Why have we allowed and produced so much bad fruit? I refer you again to look up 2 Timothy 3:1-5 where Paul describes the character of the last days church.

> Now I [God] will tell you what I am going to do to my vineyard: I will take away its hedge, and it will be destroyed; I will break down its wall, and it will be trampled. I will make it a wasteland, neither pruned nor cultivated, and briars and thorns will grow there. I will command the clouds not to rain on it. (Isaiah 5:5-6)

In these verses, Isaiah describes the consequences of producing bad fruit (heart characteristics) when the Israelites were so abundantly blessed to produce good fruit (spiritual). The hedge, or protection God granted His people, will be removed and destroyed. Israel experienced God's judgment as promised. This principle still applies. I believe that the freedoms the church in America now enjoys will be taken away because of our

carelessness and irresponsibility. We have not been committed to using these freedoms to teach and to live for
God according to His righteousness. As in the days of
Noah, holy fear of God's standards has been mostly
replaced by worldly freedom to think as you want.
Besides losing God's covering, the church will experience "a lack of rain" meaning God's nourishment will be
removed.

Isaiah warns the Israelites through the use of the
descriptive words in these verses. Isaiah tells the
Israelites that Jerusalem will become a barren wasteland
because of the people's sin. Thus, the church in America,
as we know it, will become a spiritual wasteland. God will
lay waste to much of the current American church structure. This will be due to the lack of commitment to His
unwavering standards and the blatant, pervasive sinfulness accepted in our nation today.

> The vineyard of the Lord Almighty is the house of Israel,
> and the men of Judah are the garden of this delight. And
> he looked for justice, but saw bloodshed; for righteous-
> ness, but heard cries of distress. (Isaiah 5:7)

The parable ends with verse seven, and Isaiah
explains that the parable refers to the house of Israel.
Israel was God's family on earth then, today it is the
church. Isaiah speaks of the Lord looking for justice
among His people, but that He saw bloodshed. The
Hebrew word used here for "bloodshed" means oppression. Just as the Israelites experienced heavy oppression
and distress because of sin, Christians in our country
today experience heavy distress. The stressful American
life-style of divorce, immorality, abortion, drug addiction, sexual permissiveness, financial snares, dishonesty,
greed, and worldly pleasure-seeking creates so much
heaviness and distress for many people.

Woe to you who add house to house and join field to field till no space is left and you live alone in the land.(Isaiah 5:8)

It appears Isaiah is referring to covetousness here. Another thought I have heard expressed about this verse is how we have built churches and more churches and added Bible study after Bible study, as if we desire ever more spiritual truth. Yet we "live alone" in that we keep God's righteous ways to ourselves. We give mental assent to the truth of God's Word but do not allow the Word of God to control our actions through our hearts. Our behavior reveals that we are hearers of the Word rather than doers.

For example, we have replaced repentance with counseling. Although we sin, we continue to live as if we were blameless. We want to believe that counseling is the only thing we need for our problems. But widespread tolerance and indifference to sin is the problem. We are all guilty and all too often refuse to admit it. It's not that I oppose counseling altogether, because I do not; I support good Christian counseling. I do believe that in most cases counseling is not enough by itself; honesty, confession, and true repentance must be a major part of the healing process.

Just as the Israelites did not see their wicked ways, neither do most of us. If I understand correctly what the Lord has shown me, God is going to perform a great act of love, and discipline America. When that happens, He will redeem us from all the defilement that separates us from one another and from Him.

The parallel I have drawn between the church and Israel should not be taken to mean that I believe the church has replaced Israel. The church is a brand new entity, composed of both Jew and Gentile. Some of the history is similar, but the Scriptures clearly teach that God's covenant with Israel is still valid. With God a promise is a promise, and a day will come (maybe soon) when the veil from Abraham's descendants will be lifted. Zechariah 12:10 informs us then the Jewish people will acknowledge that Jesus is their Messiah.

> The Lord Almighty has declared in my hearing: "Surely the great houses will become desolate, the fine mansions left without occupants. A ten-acre vineyard will produce only a bath of wine, a homer of seed only an ephah of grain."
>
> Woe to those who rise early in the morning to run after their drinks, who stay up late at night till they are inflamed with wine. They have harps and lyres and their banquets, tambourines and flutes and wine, but they have no regard for the deeds of the Lord, no respect for the work of his hands.
>
> Therefore my people will go into exile for their lack of understanding; their men of rank will die of hunger and their masses will be parched with thirst. Therefore the grave enlarges its appetite and opens its mouth without limit; into it will descend their nobles and masses with all their brawlers and revelers. So man will be brought low and mankind humbled, the eyes of the arrogant humbled.
>
> But the Lord Almighty will be exalted by his justice, and the holy God will show himself holy by his righteousness. Then sheep will graze as in their own pasture; lambs will feed among the ruins of the rich. (Isaiah 5:9-17)

Here Isaiah describes God's judgment on those who "run after their drinks"—those who chase after the ways of the world. They will go into exile. Going into exile refers to how God's people (the church) will lose their freedom when they fail to serve Him.

The following verses are a warning not to mock God and His judgment. Mockery of God was one of the sins in Noah's day, just as many people in Isaiah's day ignored his warnings.

> Woe to those who draw sin along with cords of deceit, and wickedness as with cart ropes, to those who say, "Let God

hurry, let him hasten his work so we may see it. Let it approach, let the plan of the Holy One of Israel come, so we may know it." Woe to those who call evil good and good evil, who put darkness for light and light for darkness, who put bitter for sweet and sweet for bitter. Woe to those who are wise in their own eyes and clever in their own sight. Woe to those who are heroes at drinking wine and champions at mixing drinks, who acquit the guilty for a bribe, but deny justice to the innocent.

Therefore, as tongues of fire lick up straw and as dry grass sinks down in flames, so their roots will decay and their flowers blow away like dust; for they have rejected the law of the Lord Almighty and spurned the word of the Holy One of Israel. Therefore the Lord's anger burns against his people; his hand is raised and he strikes them down. The mountains shake, and the dead bodies are like refuse in the streets. Yet for all this, his anger is not turned away, his hand is still upraised.

He lifts up a banner for the distant nations, he whistles for those at the ends of the earth. Here they come, swiftly and speedily! Not one of them grows tired or stumbles, not one slumbers or sleeps; not a belt is loosened at the waist, not a sandal thong is broken. Their arrows are sharp, all their bows are strung; their horses' hoofs seem like flint, their chariot wheels like a whirlwind. Their roar is like that of the lion, they roar like young lions; they growl as they seize their prey and carry it off with no one to rescue. In that day they will roar over it like the roaring of the sea. And if one looks at the land, he will see darkness and distress; even the light will be darkened by the clouds. (Isaiah 5:18-30)

When I finished reading this portion of Scripture, the Lord directed me to chapter three. As you read this next passage, keep in mind that Jerusalem and Judah identify the center of God's spiritual activities. In this prophecy, the principles stated would refer to the church in America as well.

See now, the Lord, the Lord Almighty, is about to take from
Jerusalem and Judah both supply and support: all supplies
of food and all supplies of water, the hero and warrior, the
judge and prophet, the soothsayer and elder, the captain of
fifty and man of rank, the counselor, skilled craftsman and
clever enchanter.

I will make boys their officials; mere children will govern
them. People will oppress each other—man against man,
neighbor against neighbor. The young will rise up against
the old, the base against the honorable.

A man will seize one of his brothers at his father's home,
and say, "You have a cloak, you be our leader; take charge
of this heap of ruins!" But in that day he will cry out, "I have
no remedy. I have no food or clothing in my house; do not
make me the leader of the people."

Jerusalem staggers, Judah is falling; their words and
deeds are against the Lord, defying his glorious presence.
The look on their faces testifies against them; they parade
their sin like Sodom [homosexuality]; they do not hide it.
Woe to them! They have brought disaster upon themselves.

**Tell the righteous it will be well with them, for they
will enjoy the fruit of their deeds.** Woe to the wicked!
Disaster is upon them! They will be paid back for what
their hands have done. Youths oppress my people,
women rule over them. O my people, your guides lead
you astray; they turn you from the path.

The Lord takes his place in court; he rises to judge the
people. The Lord enters into judgment against the elders
and leaders of his people: "It is you who have ruined my
vineyard; the plunder from the poor is in your houses.
What do you mean by crushing my people and grinding
the faces of the poor?" declares the Lord, the Lord
Almighty.

The Lord says, "The women of Zion are haughty, walking
along with outstretched necks, flirting with their eyes, trip-
ping along with mincing steps, with ornaments jingling on
their ankles. Therefore the Lord will bring sores on the
heads of the women of Zion; the Lord will make their scalps
bald." (Isaiah 3:1-17)

The women of Zion symbolize the women members of the church. Today it appears that many believe themselves to be better than others, and are caught up in the high fashions of the world.

In that day the Lord will snatch away their finery: the bangles and headbands and crescent necklaces, the earrings and bracelets and veils, the headdresses and ankle chains and sashes, the perfume bottles and charms, the signet rings and nose rings, the fine robes and the capes and cloaks, the purses and mirrors, and the linen garments and tiaras and shawls.

Instead of fragrance there will be a stench; instead of a sash, a rope; instead of well dressed hair, baldness; instead of fine clothing, sackcloth; instead of beauty, branding. Your men will fall by the sword, your warriors in battle. The gates of Zion will lament and mourn; destitute, she will sit on the ground.

In that day seven women will take hold of one man and say, "We will eat our own food and provide our own clothes; only let us be called by your name. Take away our disgrace!" (Isaiah 3:18-4:1)

After chapter three, I was directed to chapter one.

Hear, O heavens! Listen, O earth! For the Lord has spoken: "I reared children and brought them up, but they have rebelled against me. The ox knows his master, the donkey his owner's manger, but Israel does not know, my people do not understand."

Ah, sinful nation, a people loaded with guilt, a brood of evildoers, children given to corruption! They have forsaken the Lord; they have spurned the Holy One of Israel and turned their backs on him. Why should you be beaten any more? Why do you persist in rebellion? Your whole head is injured, your whole heart afflicted. From the sole of your foot to the top of your head there is no soundness — only wounds and welts and open sores, not cleansed or bandaged or soothed with oil.

Your country is desolate, your cities burned with fire;
your fields are being stripped by foreigners right before
you, laid waste as when overthrown by strangers. (Isaiah
1:2-7)

Isaiah says that even an ox recognizes its owner, but
God's family on earth (Israel then, now the church) has
forgotten. The prophet describes cities burned with fire
and fields being stripped by foreigners. Think of the drug
and crime infested turmoil within our inner cities
today—it's worse than a raging fire. Our fields are being
ravaged by foreigners in the sense that America's real
estate is increasingly bought out from under us by foreign investors.

The Daughter of Zion is left like a shelter in a vineyard,
like a hut in a field of melons, like a city under siege.
Unless the Lord Almighty had left us some survivors, we
would have become like Sodom, we would have been like
Gomorrah. Hear the word of the Lord, you rulers of
Sodom; listen to the law of our God, you people of
Gomorrah! "The multitude of your sacrifices—what are
they to me?" says the Lord. "I have more than enough of
burnt offerings, of rams and the fat of fattened animals; I
have no pleasure in the blood of bulls and lambs and
goats. When you come to appear before me, who has
asked this of you, this trampling of my courts? Stop
bringing meaningless offerings! Your incense is
detestable to me. New Moons, Sabbaths and convoca-
tions—I cannot bear your evil assemblies. Your New
Moon festivals and your appointed feasts my soul hates.
They have become a burden to me; I am weary of bearing
them. When you spread out your hands in prayer, I will
hide my eyes from you; even if you offer many prayers, I
will not listen. Your hands are full of blood; wash and
make yourselves clean. Take your evil deeds out of my
sight! Stop doing wrong, learn to do right! Seek justice,
encourage the oppressed. Defend the cause of the fatherless, plead the case of the widow.

"Come now, let us reason together," says the Lord. "Though your sins are like scarlet, they shall be as white as snow; though they are red as crimson, they shall be like wool. If you are willing and obedient, you will eat the best from the land; but if you resist and rebel, you will be devoured by the sword." For the mouth of the Lord has spoken.

See how the faithful city [the church] has become a harlot! She once was full of justice; righteousness used to dwell in her—but now murderers! Your silver has become dross, your choice wine is diluted with water. Your rulers are rebels, companions of thieves; they all love bribes and chase after gifts. They do not defend the cause of the fatherless; the widow's case does not come before them. Therefore the Lord, the Lord Almighty, the Mighty One of Israel, declares: "Ah, I will get relief from my foes and avenge myself on my enemies. I will turn my hand against you; I will thoroughly purge away your dross and remove your impurities. I will restore your judges as in days of old, your counselors as at the beginning. Afterward you will be called The City of Righteousness, the Faithful City."

Zion will be redeemed with justice, her penitent ones with righteousness. But rebels and sinners will both be broken, and those who forsake the Lord will perish. You will be ashamed because of the sacred oaks in which you have delighted; you will be disgraced because of the gardens that you have chosen. You will be like an oak with fading leaves, like a garden without water. The mighty man will become tinder and his work a spark; both will burn together, with no one to quench the fire. (Isaiah 1:8-31)

I then was led to read Isaiah chapter two, beginning with verse six.

You have abandoned your people, the house of Jacob. They are full of superstitions from the East; they practice divination like the Philistines and clasp hands with pagans.

Their land is full of silver and gold (wealth); there is no end to their treasures. Their land is full of horses; there is no end to their chariots [automobiles, today's means of transportation]. Their land is full of idols [material attachments]; they bow down to the work of their own hands, to what their fingers have made. So man will be brought low and mankind humbled—but do not forgive them.

Go into the rocks, hide in the ground from the dread of the Lord and the splendor of his majesty! The eyes of the arrogant man will be humbled and the pride of men brought low; the Lord alone will be exalted in that day.

The Lord Almighty has a day in store for all the proud and lofty, for all that is exalted (and they will be humbled), for all the cedars of Lebanon, tall and lofty, and all the oaks of Bashan, for all the towering mountains and all the high hills, for every lofty tower and every fortified wall, for every trading ship and every stately vessel. The arrogance of man will be brought low and the pride of men humbled; the Lord alone will be exalted in that day, and the idols will totally disappear.

Men will flee to caves in the rocks and to holes in the ground from dread of the Lord and the splendor of his majesty, when he rises to shake the earth. In that day men will throw away to the rodents and bats their idols of silver and idols of gold, which they made to worship. They will flee to caverns in the rocks and to the overhanging crags from dread of the Lord and the splendor of his majesty, when he rises to shake the earth. Stop trusting in man, who has but a breath in his nostrils. Of what account is he? (Isaiah 2:6-22)

The preceding verses describe God's coming judgment. However, God never leaves us without hope. Finally, I was led to read the first five verses of chapter two, followed by chapter four verses two through six. This portion of Scripture foretells the reign of Christ.

This is what Isaiah son of Amoz saw concerning Judah and Jerusalem: In the last days the mountain of the

Lord's temple will be established as chief among the mountains; it will be raised above the hills, and all nations will stream to it.

Many peoples will come and say, "Come, let us go up to the mountain of the Lord, to the house of the God of Jacob. He will teach us his ways, so that we may walk in his paths."

The law will go out from Zion, the word of the Lord from Jerusalem. He will judge between the nations and will settle disputes for many peoples. They will beat their swords into plowshares and their spears into pruning hooks. Nation will not take up sword against nation, nor will they train for war anymore. Come, O house of Jacob, let us walk in the light of the Lord.

In that day the Branch of the Lord will be beautiful and glorious, and the fruit of the land will be the pride and glory of the survivors in Israel. Those who are left in Zion, who remain in Jerusalem, will be called holy, all who are recorded among the living in Jerusalem. The Lord will wash away the filth of the women of Zion; he will cleanse the bloodstains from Jerusalem [includes the church] by a spirit of judgment and a spirit of fire. Then the Lord will create over all of Mount Zion and over those who assemble there a cloud of smoke by day and a glow of flaming fire by night; over all the glory will be a canopy. It will be shelter and shade from the heat of the day, and a refuge and hiding place from the storm and rain. (Isaiah 2:1-5; 4:2-6)

I have shared what the Lord has revealed to my heart. Though I know what I have said is the truth, there will be those who disagree. Some will argue that these Scriptures apply only to Israel, and that I mistakenly believe that the Lord instructed me to use them to reveal judgment on the church in America. Whether you believe they apply to the church in America or not, be wise and be alert. Seek God, His righteousness, and commit to the Lord Jesus Christ with all your heart. There shouldn't be any disagreement about that.

It will never be more important to walk in holy fear and live for righteousness than in the days to come. The days ahead will require all Christians to develop patient endurance and demonstrate faithfulness. For the faithful and those who seek to walk in righteousness, the days to come will be a time of great revival. As Isaiah writes in 3:10: "Tell the righteous, it will be well with them, for they will enjoy the fruits of their deeds." They will "go out with joy, and be led forth with peace..." (Isaiah 55:12).

The church in America has been under tremendous spiritual attack as I have discussed. It needs help desperately; a lot of spiritual help. To those who believe themselves to be spiritual, now is not the time to feel superior because we possess some knowledge of God or have spiritual gifts. Now is the time to swallow our spiritual pride, to humbly seek God and His righteousness, to have a repentant heart, to put on the full armor of God, resist the enemy and his deceitful tactics, and cry out to the Lord for His mercy and direction.

> Gather together, gather together, O shameful nation, before the appointed time arrives and that day sweeps on like chaff, before the fierce anger of the Lord comes upon you, before the day of the Lord's wrath comes upon you. Seek the Lord, all you humble of the land, you who do what he commands. Seek righteousness, seek humility; perhaps you will be sheltered on the day of the Lord's anger. (Zephaniah 2:1-3)

WHEN WILL JUDGMENT OCCUR?

The judgment described in these chapters of Isaiah is coming, but I do not know when all of these things will take place. As was true of God's warning to the Israelites, His timing is not foretold. What I do know for sure is that it will happen. There is too much evil in America today for God to ignore it. The church has continued to shrink in influence, and the people of the world feel free to do anything that comes to mind. I also believe I know *how* this judgment will occur. It is prophesied in Revelation 13. The American life style as we know it will collapse due to a profound, but little noticed, flaw in its economic structure. As our economy falters, the beast system will begin to increase its control over buying and selling. Few will resist such intervention. On the contrary, many people will demand government control. They will cry out to the government to fill their needs. As for Christians, it will be a time of purging us from mixing so heavily with the world system; a time of separation from worldly entrapment. It will be a time of revival brought about by widespread personal economic failure.

Chapter 7

SPECIAL ECONOMIC REPORT

The stock market crash of October 19, 1987, seems to have come and gone without serious fallout. At the time, many people expressed great concern. That is because the crash sent a clear message of extreme financial and economic vulnerability. No matter what triggered this Black Monday, if our financial markets were sound, a plunge of this speed and magnitude could not have happened. Do you remember those fearful moments after you first heard the news? One of our country's spiritual leaders, David Wilkerson, later wrote:

I WAS AT THE STOCK EXCHANGE ON WALL STREET WHEN THE CRASH CAME! I was there because the Holy Spirit prompted me to go. On Sunday night, the day before the crash, I stood in Times Square and warned, "If you want to see history being made, go down to Wall Street tomorrow! I'm going down there because prophecy is going to be fulfilled to the letter!"

It was frightful! ... To see it firsthand was terrifying. The cursing, the anger, the disbelief, was astounding. Everybody was stunned. I watched brokers coming out of the exchange to get some fresh air, and they shook their heads in disbelief—some with eyes glistened with tears.

I sat on the stairs across from the exchange, watching the panic grow—and the Spirit of the Lord moved me profoundly. I heard, so clearly, in my inner man, "God has had enough! Enough of the greed, the arrogance and pride—and now great tribulations will accelerate! It will never be 'normal' again! America and the world is racing toward the final reckoning!"

Suddenly, great peace flooded my soul, and I wept inwardly—because of the joy of the Lord! God whispered to my heart, "I am God of the highs and the lows. What is happening here on Wall Street has nothing to do with you or with any who trust in me! I will be faithful, no matter what happens—even if the entire system collapses. Be not afraid."[1]

The stock market has regained what it lost that day, but I believe that Black Monday 1987 is a sign of the economic times. It is a warning. The failure of the savings-and-loans is another. The bailout will exceed $500 billion. Now, banks are failing at an alarming rate, corporate bankruptcies are on the increase, and major insurance companies show signs of distress. The fear has subsided for the time being, but it will return with the next economic calamity.

The crash was merely one of several indications that something is terribly wrong with our economy. There is an underlying structural problem, a problem that appears to be irreversible. I believe that judgment may come about through economic disaster. Major economic collapse may be God's way of bringing about the coming judgment of America.

FROM PROSPERITY TO HEAVY DEBT

To understand our current financial troubles, it's necessary to go back to the 1940s. World War II left the nations of Europe and the Pacific Rim in shambles. Many people lost their homes, but they lost their means of

livelihood as well. The fighting destroyed factories, busi-
nesses, power plants, roads, bridges, rail lines and more.
Germany, England, Japan, and many other nations lost
their industrial capacity. The infrastructure needed for
economic productivity had been wiped out. At the same
time, these nations lost a whole generation of industrial
and government managers. The leadership necessary for
business enterprise took a serious blow. Consequently,
the economic strength of these nations experienced a
severe economic setback. England, for example, has
never really recovered. Rationing of food, oil, and other
staple commodities continued for years after the war. It
went from an industrial power with globe encircling
interests to a declining nation with a modest role in international affairs.

But while the European and Pacific powers crawled
out from under the rubble, the United States was well on
its way to economic supremacy. World War II *enhanced*
America's fortunes. None of the fighting had occurred on
American soil, so the United States emerged as the only
major power with its industrial and agricultural base
intact. Wartime production pulled the domestic economy out of the Depression, and a wide sector of the
economy never demobilized. U.S. workers made huge
economic gains. Few of those in the industrial world
could boast higher pay, more extensive fringe benefits,
or better working conditions. Production within
American factories continued at a steady clip as the
United States was in a unique position to furnish its
wartime allies and enemies with many of the products
and services their people needed. During the next 30
years, American products achieved a worldwide reputation.

The postwar years gave American companies a tremendous headstart. The lack of foreign competition
combined with Yankee know-how catapulted the United

States to leadership in many economic sectors. The United States captured first place in the production of automobiles, machine tools, electronic equipment and other vital industries. American factories became models of industrial excellence as American technology and management expertise set the standard. Not surprisingly, few Americans wanted to buy foreign products. American consumers refused foreign imports, which they badmouthed as shoddy imitations. We preferred high quality domestic products to second rate goods manufactured abroad. This created an impressive trade surplus. Year after year, Americans sold far more than they bought, and billions of excess dollars poured into the U.S. economy. We provided the major share of the goods and services needed around the world.

As a result, the American standard of living shot up beyond imagination. Americans claimed vast worldly possessions unprecedented in world history. With less than 7 percent of the world's population, we accumulated half of the world's wealth and consumed a full third of the world's resources each year. American factories churned out top quality products, and thick-walleted American consumers snapped them up. Americans, because they earned high wages, could purchase the steady flow of products from domestic factories. This availability of consumer goods allowed Americans to live better than virtually every other people throughout the world. Those categorized as "poor" in America would have made the "upper class" in many countries. The American life style became the envy of the world as Americans routinely enjoyed products and services completely out of reach for people in other lands.

But then, the tide began to turn. The military obligations the United States had incurred around the globe following the war meant massive government spending. The American economy became dependent on foreign oil, and the oil producing nations organized to charge more. American industries lost their technological edge. More important, the rest of the world regained its industrial capacity. European and Asian competitors caught up, and began to pass us within industries pioneered in the United States. They had developed efficient production methods and rigid quality control standards. Imported clothing, Asian electronic goods, and foreign cars meant value for the American consumer. And for the first time in half a century, Americans began buying more than they were selling. Rather than a healthy trade surplus, we generated a massive trade deficit.

Now we find ourselves in a difficult financial situation. We should scale down our standard of living to meet our diminished economic position in the world, but we are not doing so. In fact, Americans expectations have *increased,* not decreased. Using the generation born after the war as a benchmark, Americans have gotten used to the idea of living with more, even though we already enjoy a standard of living unknown before. For some, it's a matter of greed. They already have more than people almost everywhere in the world, but still they are not satisfied. They want a more comfortable house, a flashier car, even trendier clothes. But for most Americans, I believe it's a matter of ignoring economic reality. Most of us have grown accustomed to the material possessions that make up what we call "the good life." Few seem to realize that they are victims of a worldly deception that ensnares people through irresistible advertising and product availability. We claim as our birthright a standard of living that took a world war to bring about. We have been led to expect a life style that's getting harder and harder to achieve.

The widening gap between expectations and capabilities has led to new dependence on credit. Without the billions of dollars exports pumped into the economy, the only way to finance our living standard is to borrow. Buying on credit is the only way for many Americans to get what they need—or are enticed by the world-system to want. Few understand the reality of this nation's economic position vis-a-vis the rest of the world. We are falling into heavy debt. Personal debt has reached a record high, savings an all-time low. Government is in the same boat. In order to maintain the services people believe they are entitled to, cities, states, and the federal government must borrow. Credit has put a stranglehold on our economy. The ability to borrow drives consumer spending, business expansion, and government services. As a consequence, the United States is in debt. Serious debt.

THE ECONOMIC BLACK HOLE

In America, economic reality means indebtedness. It would be convenient to ignore this, but the consequences of our nation's reversal of fortune since the 1940s is inescapable. During the 1980s, our country shifted from being the largest creditor nation in the world to being the largest debtor nation. People face huge personal debt. Corporations juggle massive business debt. Government operates with huge deficits. Exactly how bad is the debt problem?

Federal Government Debt

Consider the federal deficit first. We have had enormous federal budget deficits since 1980. U.S. government debt more than tripled from $800 billion at the beginning of 1980 to over $3 trillion by the end of 1990. Do you know what that means? It means the national government racked up over twice as much debt in a single decade—the 1980s—than it had accumulated during the previous 200 years of our country's history. The interest alone on that debt amounts to a full third of the annual budget. About $832 million a day is spent on interest that does not buy a thing. It is the single largest expense in the national budget. A balanced budget is out of the realm of possibility. "Balanced budget" sounds as antiquated to government accountants as the adding machine. In a recent Congressional debate, Dale Bumpers, an Arkansas Democrat, said, "Interest payments on the debt will be bigger than any other item in the federal budget forever. Forever."

Foreign Debt

Foreign debt is also staggering. Foreign debt—that's the amount the United States owes to other countries—jumped to $400 billion between 1979 and 1990. Who loans us this money? Our former enemy Japan is a significant source. It's ironic that our way of life now depends on the willingness of the Japanese to help finance it. They have the money to loan in part because we buy so much more from them than they buy from us. The trade deficit—the amount we import over what we export—has added over $160 billion in some years to our foreign debt total.

Third World Debt

Then there is Third World debt. This is the amount of money less developed nations owe the industrial nations. Collectively, Mexico, Brazil and other countries owe over a trillion dollars to U.S. banks. The economic fortunes of First World nations depend on whether or not Third World nations pay up. Increasing fear that they will default on these loans imperils the international financial system as well as political stability in the underdeveloped countries. A large portion of less developed countries debt is already in default, and as a greater portion of these loans fall into default, America's economy will weaken even further. U.S. banks will be forced to write off more loans and increase reserves, further jeopardizing their capital and earnings.

Consumer Debt

Now consider a kind of indebtedness that's closer to home. Since 1982, U.S. economic growth has been fueled by consumer debt. We, the consumers, have gone on an unprecedented spending spree. Outstanding consumer debt was $296 billion in 1982. At the end of 1990, it reached $800 billion. In economic terms, the American consumer is dangerously exposed with very little cash equity. The "spirit of merchandising" has grabbed people's hearts and caused staggering debt. Many American families depend on two incomes to meet their debt obligations; the loss of one income even for a brief period would tilt them dangerously close to financial ruin. Needless to say, millions of Americans will be in serious financial trouble with a decline in the economy and rising unemployment. Nearly a million families filed for personal bankruptcy in 1990, a 50 percent increase over 1989.

Business Debt

In addition to government and personal debt, there's business debt. Business debt rose from $1.3 trillion in 1982 to nearly $8 trillion by 1990. It's the U.S. government, specifically, the Federal Reserve, that finances this debt. In recent years the Federal Reserve has increased the money supply, that is, the amount of money it prints, at the fastest pace since World War II. During one recent six year period, Money Stock (MI) rose over 50 percent.

THE COMING CRISIS

David Wilkerson, Pat Robertson, and other spiritual leaders state that the debt-ridden U.S. economy has reached the point of no return. Americans have dug themselves a financial hole so deep they will never climb out. Sooner than later, the system will have reached that critical point when the rising debt collides with falling earnings. When the right portion of debt goes unpaid, the credit system that drives our economy will falter. This impending financial crisis will have profound social and spiritual consequences.

Beyond the Great Depression

By supplying the rest of the world with many of its goods and services after World War II, Americans were able to enjoy a standard of living that was unheard of before. We have artificially maintained this living standard in recent years through credit. The insurmountable debt that has resulted casts a gloomy shadow over America's economic future.

Few politicians and corporate chieftains seem willing to admit there is a problem. Government officials and business leaders carry on as if nothing is wrong. In the rosy forecasts given by vested interest groups, the U.S. economy will rebound. In reality, it's more vulnerable to complete collapse than ever before. The years of unconscious overspending cannot be eradicated. No matter what the politicians promise, record indebtedness will ultimately result in financial judgment.

In a larger sense, what the government does or doesn't do at this point won't make much difference. Current "solutions" to the debt crisis amount to economic fiction rather than sound economic thinking. Take the idea of consumer spending. The notion is that the economy will be healthy as long as consumer spending remains strong. In other words, everybody will be poorer unless people spend more than they can afford. Does that make sense to you? Pat Robertson, President of Christian Broadcasting Network, explains what Uncle Sam has been up to:

> This year [1991], although the Federal Government claims it will raise no new taxes, state and local governments will add some $25 billion in taxes, the higher

social security taxes all workers pay amount to back-to-back $25 billion annual tax increases, and the Post Office added a 16 percent increase in its rates. Perversely, postal rate hikes, state sales taxes, and the federal luxury tax are all figured into inflation growth figures which the Federal Reserve Board has been choking the money supply to fight.

During this fiscal year, the federal government will be spending at least $300 billion more than it takes in, yet the money supply has been allowed to grow by an anemic $102 billion. The excess will be paid for by selling government bonds, which in turn will drain $200 billion from business investment, real estate, consumer spending, and the stock market.[2]

We will not be able to spend our way out of this crisis—that's the bottom line. Whether consumers spend more, or spend less; whether the government taxes more, or taxes less, the debt will continue to grow. Traditional methods taken to prop up the economy simply are not feasible. No conventional solutions are available because this is an unheard of economic problem.

Circumstances are right for major economic collapse. Pat Robertson warns of a gigantic "debt implosion":

"A worldwide economic collapse is extremely likely in the next few years. Those unprepared may stand naked before a crisis unseen in the United States since the Civil War."

Those words appeared in a recent letter of the prestigious World Future Society, whose directors contain some of the nation's most industrious leaders. They see, as I do, that the world's gigantic $25 trillion debt, the billions of square feet of debt-financed empty office buildings, the wildly inflated stock markets of some nations, the S&L crisis, the insurance crisis—coupled with the inability of the U.S. to balance either its budget or its trade—will sooner or later set off a debt implosion.

When that happens, wealth just disappears. Stock values collapse, bonds lose value, weak companies go out of business, real estate values collapse for lack of buyers, financial institutions fail, bank CDs and money market funds can drop in value, unemployment soars, and government revenues fall dramatically while welfare spending rises.

Then there follows a serious depression with enormous human suffering, when prices fall and those with money or credit can buy undreamed of bargains in goods and services. Or, as an alternative, governments will try to finance recovery schemes by printing money. Hyperinflation follows and the prices of everything tangible goes into orbit. Hyperinflation devastates the elderly on fixed incomes and all those who have been frugal and saved their money. In Germany, hyperinflation wiped out the middle class, devastated the nation, and set the stage for Adolph Hitler.

This debt implosion could take place at any time, but my prayerfully-considered view is that it will take place after the 1992 elections, probably in 1993. We have been having successive financial shocks for the past two years— the collapse of junk bonds, the collapse of Third World debt, the collapsing economy of the Soviet Union, the collapse of the S&Ls, the collapse of high-visibility insurance companies, massive foreclosure of real estate, etc.

Unfortunately the problem is not over. As I have written previously, the total level of debt in our nation is now almost three times the entire output of the country. This so-called debt to G.N.P. ratio has not been this high since the Great Depression. In 1933, the government had almost no debt and was able to act as the engine of recovery. Now at the end of a decade of unparalleled prosperity, the government cannot borrow and spend anymore than it already has, nor can business borrow much more. If a depression hits in the next couple of years, the falling economy could cause our debt to G.N.P ratio to skyrocket and bring on a dollar collapse and soaring interest rates as both the government and private business would be forced to pay an increasingly higher premium to borrow against their failing credit ratings.[3]

We have mortgaged the future to pay for the present. In accumulating such terrific debt, we have chartered a course that leads from riches to rags. At the root of this economic vulnerability is our failure to live within our means. *Installment debt, mortgage debt, government debt, plus corporate debt and other private debt has risen in a vain effort to maintain our present standard of living.* Probably sooner than later, the American people will be forced to accept a dramatically different living standard.

Shock Waves

It's hard to say what will be the straw that breaks the camel's back—which shock to the economy will trigger such a major collapse. As Pat Robertson points out, there are quite a number of potential shocks.

Economics aside the world seems to be undergoing other massive strains:

Bangladesh was hit by a massive cyclone which caused untold devastation to that impoverished land. Soon thereafter the world learned that famine in Ethiopia, Somolia, and the Sudan had grown in such intensity that some 6,000,000 people were threatened with starvation.

Reports from the recent AIDS conference in Italy sent alarming news that the U.S. is spending in 1991 $5.8 billion treating those with AIDS, and that cost will leap to $10 billion by 1994. Over one million active cases of AIDS exist in Africa. AIDS is the number one killer of women 25 to 44 in New York City. This killer disease is becoming a plague of unimagined human suffering and financial consequence, yet the leaders of this world refuse to condemn the sinful source of most of its spread—homosexuality, promiscuous sex, and intravenous drug use.

In mid-June, the shocks hitting the world escalated dramatically with the eruption of a volcano that had been dormant for over 600 years, Mount Pinatubo, in the

Philippines. Some meteorologists are saying that the fine aerosol being launched by Mount Pinatubo fifteen miles into the air will cause the formation of another rapid warming of the sea water in the Pacific Ocean off South America (called El Nino—the child) which in turn would cause serious storms, floods, and drought around the world. According to the experts, there have been nine El Ninos in the last fifty years, and all but one have been preceded by a volcanic eruption in the lower latitudes.

Pinatubo is not alone. It is linked to a series of fault lines than run through Japan, up into the Aleutian Islands, and down the west coast of North America and South America—the so-called "Ring of Fire." A major disruption in the Philippines could conceivably trigger earthquakes and volcanic activities in Japan, plus the powerful earthquake that scientists have long been predicting for the Los Angeles, California area.

Could the world, already on the brink of financial collapse, cope with pervasive drought and massive crop failures, killer earthquakes in crowded urban areas, and the possible devastation by earthquakes and volcanoes of Japan, the world's second most powerful nation?[4]

NEW ECONOMIC ERA

Whether or not volcanic activity triggers it, economic collapse is bound to occur given historic indebtedness. What will happen when the living standard we have known for so long begins to evaporate? No one can predict precisely what would happen, but there could be significant social and political fallout to any major economic catastrophe.

After the Collapse

A major financial panic might bring civil disorder, violence, and unimaginable chaos. Things could get out of control, not necessarily because people lack basic necessities, but because they have been denied the things they expect to receive as American citizens. It's not the same in our country as it was during the Great Depression. During the 1930s, the majority of people were accustomed to working hard for simple necessities. The generation that survived the Depression was glad to have enough to eat, something to wear, and a roof over their heads. The "gimme generation" of the 1970s and 1980s will not be content with that.

But whether or not there are riots in streets following the impending financial crisis, *fear of* lawlessness and disorder will create an unprecedented reliance on government. As this nation's economic structure unravels, Americans will increasingly look to the government to do something. Few will resist government intervention, many will demand it. It will be easy for government leaders of the beast system to promise social order in return for absolute compliance. The government will have great incentive to eliminate perceived threats to the economy by extending control over buying and selling. When the next economic shock provokes deep-seated fear, people will cry out to the government to save them.

It is difficult to say what these commercial regulations will entail but Bible prophecy clearly points to the day when the beast (the U.S. government) will control economic transactions. A marking system of some kind will be imposed. In Revelation 13:16, John prophesies of a time when "no one can buy or sell unless he has the mark." He tied the marking system with the numbering system of the beast society as the method used for control. Did you know that a computer reads "marks" not numbers? Only by the wisdom of God could John have known this.

The Mark of the Beast

Such a marking system has already been developed. In fact, this system has operated since 1973. The UPC symbol identifies practically every item found on grocery and retail store shelves. As the *Los Angeles Times* explained it:

The grocery store industry has developed what it calls the Universal Product Code (UPC), which to the consumer looks like a series of vertical lines covering an area about the size of a large postage stamp.[5]

The purpose of the UPC bar code is to standardize product identification for use with automated cash register equipment. What is of interest from the perspective of Bible prophecy is that every UPC code contains three unidentified marks corresponding to the number 666. Students of Bible prophecy know that sixes are among the secrets of the economy destined to close out this, the Gentile Age. These three sixes are the key working numbers for every version of the UPC code. Computer experts I have consulted have told me that the triple-six pattern has become a universal design standard; it cannot be changed.

Figure 1 shows the most common UPC design. Most of the marks, or bars, in the symbol are identified by numbers at the bottom of the code. But there are always at least three unidentified bars. In this design, these marks appear on the far left, in the middle, and at the far right. Three of these unidentified marks are always the number 6. I have also included the interpretation standard (figure 2) for the bar code design so that you can check some of the bar codes found on products in your own home. You will discover three unidentified marks on any code you inspect. These marks translate into three sixes.

FIGURE 1

**MOST COMMON
UPC DESIGN**

FIGURE 2

Sets

Set #1 is designated by the number 1	INTERPRETATION
Set #2 is designated by the number 2	STANDARD FOR BAR
Set #3 is designated by the number 3	CODES

Why is the number six used in this way? Computer technicians say that 6 is the perfect computer number. Six is the perfect number because computers work on a series of six cores that allow current to change direction in order to perform switching operations. The six cores work in conjunction with 60 displacements X 6—one character—one bit of information. The formula for this system is 6 60 6. To number a card, person, or item, the transaction must be prefixed "six hundred, threescore, and six" just as John said in Revelation 13:18. Apple Computer Incorporated celebrated the number 6 as the perfect computer number when it introduced the first 200 Apple I's to be retailed for $666.66.[6]

Although the bar codes on grocery items are the most noticeable, credit and bank cards make use of bar codes, too. These are micro-encoded along the magnetic strip on the back of the card. When these marks are scanned by laser light, the optical pattern is converted to an electrical signal (analog), which is converted in turn to a digital signal, then decoded by a microprocessor. Literally tens of thousands of characters can be micro-encoded on the three by one half inch magnetic strip on a single card. A little more automation is all it would take to generate a personal record of every person's purchases, transactions, and so on.

The technology needed to limit who buys and sells already exists, and it could be used for various purposes should financial panic require strict control. A well tested international marking system is already in place. It represents a ready-made marking system for the government to utilize in order to implement the mark of the beast John describes (Revelation, 13:16-18).

If the Christian community recognized the government effort to control trade as the mark of the beast, there would likely be some opposition. Some Christians know from reading the book of Revelation that they should not accept the number of the beast. Perhaps Christians would refuse to accept the mark, and still be able to buy and sell at least at first. But as the months pass, then a year or two, the government's thirst for power and the public's general mistrust and suspicion will emerge. Christians, as well as others who attempt to avoid receiving the mark, will come under greater pressure to yield and become a part of the system. In my opinion, government control of the buying and selling process may be God's means of purging His people from the beast's economy. When that day comes, Christians will need to separate themselves from their dependence on the world and acknowledge their dependence on Him.

REAL FINANCIAL SECURITY

As the economic conditions described in the book of Revelation unfold in these last days, many crave financial security. I would not attempt to offer personal financial advice. Everyone's financial condition is different, plus I am not qualified to say exactly what you should or should not do with your finances. The Bible does, however, provide guidance. As Christians, we should live within our means. We need to be on guard to avoid falling prey to worldly influences. People today, especially young people, face enormous pressure to buy now, pay later. It's awfully easy to run up a large debt to get all the things available today. There is no question but what the seducing spirits have implanted a deep desire for material acquisition. But the Christian life is not about giving in to selfish desires, it's about service and devotion to Jesus.

We can learn a great deal from the Lord's counsel to the church at Laodicea (Revelation 3:14-22). The Laodicean church typifies so much of the thinking in contemporary Christianity today. They were a self-satisfied, self-righteous group. They sought to fulfill their own interests and since they were satisfied, nothing else mattered. The Laodiceans were full of hypocrisy; they were deceiving those around them with outward appearances. Jesus gave them some "financial advice":

> You say, "I am rich; I have acquired wealth and do not need a thing." But you do not realize that you are wretched, pitiful, poor, blind and naked. I counsel you to buy from me gold refined in the fire, so you can become rich; and white clothes to wear, so you can cover your shameful nakedness; and salve to put on your eyes, so you can see. (Revelation 3:17-18)

What did Jesus mean when he advised them to "buy from me gold refined in the fire, so you can become rich"? He was not talking about the kind of gold stored at Fort Knox, of course. He was talking about becoming spiritually rich. The only way to buy the kind of gold Jesus talks about is through total commitment.

When the subject of total commitment is discussed in Christian circles, many Christians feel the need to be involved in some activity. Our society trains us to have confidence in the things we can accomplish by our own willpower. Christians go to extremes to carry out tasks of a fleshly nature by making up rules and regulations believing that this is total commitment. Yet with all our physical efforts we do not have spiritual victory. Victory means overcoming sin and the self-centered ways of the world.

We are defeated precisely because we try to understand and commit in activities of the flesh that which is of a spiritual nature. Commitment to the Lord Jesus Christ is not something of the flesh, but of the spirit; it is of the heart. Therefore, we cannot apply our normal approach of using human wisdom and human understanding in this area (see John 3:6). Spiritual commitment must come from our inner being. Our bodies, minds, personalities, natural talents and abilities, when yielded to Him become the vehicles through which He works His will. "For it is God who works in you to will and to act according to his good purpose" (Philippians 2:13). Deep commitment in our hearts means giving ourselves—our total being—as a living sacrifice to God so He and His indwelling Spirit are in control.

Many Christians are *involved* today but that does not mean they are *committed*; there is a vast difference between the two. It is easy to be involved because involvement is basically activity. We can be active in a church doing many works in the name of Jesus but that does not mean that we are necessarily committed to Him and the characteristics of His teachings. Remember the Pharisees? What about some of the clergy today? Total commitment is when our activity requires sacrificing all personal benefit for the glory of God. Paul says:

> I appeal to you therefore, brethren, and beg of you in view of [all] the mercies of God, to make a decisive dedication of your bodies—presenting all your members and faculties—as a living sacrifice, holy (devoted, consecrated) and well pleasing to God, which is your reasonable (rational, intelligent) service and spiritual worship.
>
> Do not be conformed to this world—this age, fashioned after and adapted to its external, superficial customs. But be transformed (changed) by the [entire]

renewal of your mind— by its new ideals and its new attitude—so that you may prove [for yourselves] what is the
good and acceptable and perfect will of God. (Romans
12:1-2, Amplified)

Spiritual commitment requires sacrifice. We are to sacrifice our selfish lives, our rights, our independence and
our individualism to the cross. It may be frightening to
give up everything to do the will of God. But in His kingdom, we give up the endless struggle for security in the
world for the inner joy and abiding peace found in only
Him.

Then he [Jesus] said to them all: "If anyone would come
after me, he must deny himself and take up his cross
daily and follow me. For whoever wants to save his life
will lose it, but whoever loses his life for me will save it."
(Luke 9:23-24)

ESCAPING THE TURMOIL

One way to deal with the reality of our failing economy
is to believe that Christians will escape. According to the
doctrine of the pre-tribulation rapture, Christians will be
whisked away before the real trouble starts. As I discuss
in the chapter that follows, my study of this subject does
not allow me to accept this sequence of events. I believe
that God will use the dire economic circumstances to
come as a means of preparing the Bride of Christ for the
second coming of Jesus. Desperate circumstances will
forge a remnant of committed Christians. Only those
Christians willing to risk everything will choose to avoid
the mark of the beast. The formation of this remnant will
be one of the ways that God will answer the many
prayers being lifted up by thousands of Christians in this
nation wanting a great move by the Holy Spirit for
revival.

Chapter 8

THE PRE-TRIBULATION RAPTURE

The doctrine of a pre-tribulation "rapture" of the saints is of concern to all Christians who are looking for the return of our Lord Jesus. I do not choose to make it a major issue, but it does need to be addressed. Consider these words by Bob Summers, from his book, *Outback with Jesus:*

In my work, I had interviewed noble Christian apostles from behind the Iron Curtain, those from Germany who survived Nazism, a woman from China who survived a mass butchering of Christians which Watchman Nee once pastored. (Watchman Nee himself died in a Communist jail in 1972.) All these believers witnessed with the same urgency: *"Go back and warn Americans that their moment is coming! Tell them they must get tougher—spiritually. And please tell them to stop preaching non-tribulation doctrines of escapism!"*

I used to shrug off such witnesses as false prophets. But in Jerusalem I took the time to discuss this issue with Corrie ten Boom, an old saint from Holland, whose story is told in *The Hiding Place* (Chosen Books). She answered decisively, gesturing with her little bony fingers as she talked, "Don't listen to these false prophets who come in the name of Jesus declaring that believers will not suffer tribulation!" (Notice who calls who *false*?) "Go back and tell your American friends that the rapture-before-tribulation doctrine is now an exclusive American message. It is not found in the rest of the nations. Christians the world over are *already* entering into tribulation!" Corrie emphasized this point before she continued, "I have been in many countries—China, for one—where the Christians were told, Don't worry. Don't worry. You will be translated, raptured, before the tribulation comes. Then when terrible persecution came, the Christians were left scattered, tortured, and broken. The few survivors felt that God had forgotten His promise to come get them. A bishop from China later told me, 'Corrie, we failed God. We should have made the people strong for persecution rather than telling them Jesus would take them away from tribulation.'" Did Jesus say in the world ye have no tribulation?

Let's face it. One cannot easily shake off her warning. After all, Corrie ten Boom should know more about tribulation than all the best-selling prophecy writers in America. She has led an extraordinary Christian life. Her entire family was placed in a Nazi concentration camp because of their love and aid for Christians and Jews. Some of the family did not come out alive. All suffered severe persecution and much torture. I am convinced Corrie knows more of the deeper meaning of costly discipleship than does the Christian profiteer who sells his bumper stickers: IN CASE OF RAPTURE THIS CAR WILL BE UNMANNED.

I am led to agree with Corrie ten Boom that easy Christianity is indeed now a uniquely American doctrine. This becomes more obvious whenever I cover the almost theatrical appearances of contemporary American prophets. They arrive at the stage entrances of convention halls in chauffeured limousines. They speak a few words, autograph books, and leave with a nice honorarium check in hand.

Who is right? Christians abroad say, "The cost of discipleship is going up!" At home, the message of "pop" prophets follows a best-selling book market trend which suggests this generation of American Christians is tribulation exempt. Who is listening to what the Spirit is saying? So much of the current teaching simply does not lend itself to alert living.

It was with a twinkle in his eye that a foreign brother told me recently, "Any prophecy book which 'proves' that American Christians are given the all-clear signal on dangerous tribulations should at least insist they remain on alert, *in case that signal was wrong.*"[1]

In this chapter, I examine the history of the pre-tribulation doctrine and review the scriptural support for this doctrine. Before I do that, I want you to understand something. I do not question the teaching of a rapture (calling up of the saints) as stated in 1 Thessalonians 4:16,17. That is a biblical fact. The material I present has to do with *when* this rapture will take place, before the tribulation—called pre-tribulation—or after the tribulation.

HISTORICAL ORIGINS OF THE PRE-TRIBULATION RAPTURE

The teaching that Christians will be caught up to heaven before the reign of the "beast" (often called anti-Christ) or the "Great Tribulation," did not appear in church history until the 1800s. The doctrine of the pre-tribulation rapture was not part of the teachings by the early church fathers, nor later church writers down through the Middle Ages. Until the early nineteenth century, it was understood that the church—the Bride of Christ—in the last days would remain here on earth through the reign of the anti-Christ and the tribulation.[2]

Now just because Christians had not heard of a pre-tribulation rapture, and therefore did not believe in this doctrine until the nineteenth century, does not mean that it's not true. The Word of God, not history or tradition, is our sole standard of truth. Nevertheless, before examining the pre-tribulation rapture teaching in light of Scripture, it is worthwhile to discover the historical beginnings of this concept.

Emanuel Lacunza

Did you know that the pre-tribulation rapture concept germinated in the Jesuit sect of the Roman church? During the Dark Ages, the Jesuits were among the most unscrupulous men on earth. A religious order founded by Loyola, they were formed to undo the work of the Reformation. The Spanish Inquisition (1478) and the massacre of St. Bartholomew (1572) represent two of their "successes." Thousands of Christians died for their faith at the hands of these men.[3]

During the fifteenth and sixteenth centuries, the Jesuits use of treachery and violence often made orderly, peaceable government impossible. So, they were expelled from many countries. Nearly a hundred decrees were issued by various governments for their expulsion. The Jesuit group expelled from Chile included a Chilean named Emanuel Lacunza. He became a member of the Jesuit order in 1747 at the age of sixteen and rose to a powerful position in the ecclesiastical hierarchy. As Superintendent of the Novitiates, he trained new recruits zealously, indoctrinating them in the principles of Jesuitry. He settled in northern Italy, and there he devoted the remainder of his life to writing a book about Jesuit doctrine.

In *The Coming of the Messiah in Glory and Majesty,* Lacunza placed end time events within current Jesuit teaching. In order to make room for all of the events he anticipated at the coming of Christ, he conceived the idea that there would have to be a period of time between the calling up of the saints and the actual appearance of the Messiah in His Glory. He wrote:

> When the Lord returns from heaven to earth, upon His coming forth from heaven, and much before His arrival at the earth, He will give His orders, and send forth His command as King and God omnipotent: "With a shout (in the Vulgate jussu, i.e. "by the order") with the voice of the archangel, and with the trump of God." At this voice of the Son of God, those who shall hear it, shall forthwith arise, as saith the evangelist St. John (chapter 5:25) "those who hear shall live."[4]

This is the germ from which sprang the concept that Christ was to come "twice," once for His saints, and again sometime later with His saints.

Lacunza wrote under the pen name of Rabbi Ben Ezra. It is likely that you have never heard of Lacunza before, but if you study prophecy, perhaps you have heard the name Ben Ezra. Many people have thought he was a Christian Jew. Apparently, this is what Lacunza wanted people to think—he chose the name for a pseudonym. He hoped his writings would gain acceptance in the Protestant world. He wanted his Jesuit principles to infiltrate Christianity.[5]

Had Lacunza lived to see his work made public, he might have been able to guarantee that the world would never know the secret of its authorship. But Lacunza was found dead on the morning of June 17, 1801, by the riverside where he was accustomed to go for a walk. The cause of death is unknown.

His book, or rather, two small volumes that represent an abridgment of it, first appeared on the Spanish Isle of Leon in 1812. In 1816, the diplomatic agent of the Republic of Buenos Aires in London published a four-volume edition of Lacunza's complete work (apparently the first complete edition). The secret of the real authorship of the work, though still hidden from the world at that time, must have been known to those concerned in this publication. Otherwise, why would the diplomatic agent of this South American Republic be interested in publishing a book when ninety-five percent of South Americans could not read? Especially the work of an author presumed to be a converted Jew—why publish it? In the early 1800s, the printing process—typesetting, press work, folding, binding—all had to be done by hand. The production of books in London was only a fraction of what it is today. Therefore, a four-volume theological work in Spanish was an important undertaking. It must have attracted great attention.

Only a handful of people in England at that time could read Spanish, so the number of copies was small and the cost correspondingly high. One library in London, however, could not afford to be without a copy of this new publication. It was a theological library, second to none in England (with the possible exception of the great university libraries of Oxford and Cambridge). This library was that of the Archbishop of Canterbury, maintained not only for the Archbishop's use, but for the English people and the church. Lacunza's four volumes were soon added to this collection.

In 1826 or so, a decade after the publication of Lacunza's work, Dr. Maitland startled the Protestant world with some of Lacunza's ideas about prophecy. Maitland, librarian to the Archbishop of Canterbury, propounded the theories of the Jesuits in a series of pamphlets on prophecy. Quite possibly, Dr. Maitland was unaware that his teachings were of Jesuit origin. He probably thought he was reading the teachings of a converted Jew named Rabbi Ben Ezra.[6]

The Irvingites

What many believed to be the wonderful Spanish writings of Rabbi Ben Ezra attracted so much attention in

London that a decision was made to translate the work into English. The task of translating Lacunza's book fell to a young Scottish Presbyterian minister named Edward Irving. Irving, reportedly brilliant but erratic, had been assistant to the great Dr. Chalmers in Glasgow. He had gone to London as a minister of the Scots church there. Irving founded the Irvingites, or as they now call themselves, the Catholic Apostolic church. Some of their practices are distinctly traceable to the views Irving imbibed from Lacunza.[7]

It is Irving that supplies the few biographical details about Lacunza. In connection with his English translation, Irving searched for information about the life of Rabbi Ben Ezra. The sponsors of Lacunza's Spanish edition of 1816 must have thought that the reputation of the book was established sufficiently to make it safe to divulge its real authorship. What Irving was able to learn about Lacunza's career he published in the preface of his translation even though the translated work still carried the pen name of Rabbi Ben Ezra.

The Brethren Movement

Besides the Irvingites, there were other Protestant movements that were influenced by Jesuit doctrines. The Tractarian movement and the Oxford movement, for example, developed in England around the early 1800s and displayed Lacunza-inspired teachings. But it was in Ireland that the pre-tribulation rapture doctrine found its greatest following. It began with the Brethren Movement and soon developed into an accepted doctrine.[8]

Serving and Waiting, the magazine of the Philadelphia School of the Bible, ran a series of articles in 1925 on "The Brethren Movement" by Harry A. Ironside, who later became pastor of Moody Church in Chicago. At that time, Dr. Ironside had been associated with assemblies of the Brethren for nearly thirty years and had access to documents and sources of information available to few outsiders. He was, therefore, uniquely qualified to present an authentic account of Brethrenism.

Dr. Ironside mentions seven leaders of the first Brethren assembly formed in Dublin and adds: "Of these it would seem that Edward Cronin was the chosen instrument to first affect the others."[9] In other words, it was Cronin who started the meeting, and who was the real founder of Brethrenism. As Ironside described him, "Mr. Cronin was a young dental student who had been brought up as a Roman Catholic, but had been graciously enlightened by the Spirit of God through personal faith in Christ, and into the knowledge of peace with God through resting upon the atoning work of the Lord Jesus."[10]

Cronin came out of the Roman church, although he never entered the full light of Christianity enough to realize the freedom in Jesus Christ. Because Cronin did not have this spiritual understanding, the dreaded weapon of excommunication used by the Roman church in the Middle Ages also applied to the Brethren movement.

Those who really believed that the little assemblies of Brethren were *"The* church," the only true Body of Christ, faced being cut off from fellowship for provoking church leaders. The threat of excommunication gave the leaders of each assembly tremendous power, and allowed their traditions to have preeminence. Continual wrangling and hair-splitting over finer points of interpretation, followed by wholesale excommunications, pockmarked the history of this church. Dr. Ironside's melancholy record of Brethren history is filled with pictures of "assemblies like soviets" arguing and fighting.

Excommunication even extended to celebrated church leaders. Dr. Edward Cronin was excommunicated from his home assembly for fellowshipping with an assembly of Christians believed to be outside the Body of Christ. George

Mueller of Bristol's famous orphanage was excommunicated because he differed with one of the Brethren leaders, John Darby. Mueller's opposition to the new pre-tribulation rapture doctrine was a major point of contention.

Internal strife continued until rival assemblies of Brethren appeared in nearly every city. Each claimed to be *"The* Church of Christ," and refused to fellowship with churches of other denominations as well as other Brethren groups. The splintering of the Brethren movement illustrates one of Satan's chosen methods of breaking down evangelical Christianity.

This brief historical account of the Brethren movement is necessary because the pre-tribulation rapture of the saints was one of the doctrines the Brethren movement used to assert itself as the true church of Christ. Brethren leaders claimed that it came to them as divine revelation; they used it to elevate themselves above all the saints of past ages and above all the other Protestant churches.

John Darby

John N. Darby became the most prominent promoter of the pre-tribulation rapture concept. Some in the Brethren movement, and others in many Protestant circles, even venerate him as the revealer of this concept. But Darby simply borrowed this concept from Irving, and Irving from Lacunza.

According to Dr. Ironside, Darby was first introduced to the pre-tribulation rapture doctrine in 1833.[11] He writes:

> A meeting began in London in the same year [1833], through a brother that Mr. Darby met while in Oxford. Some little time before this, a group of earnest Christians had been meeting in the castle of Lady Powerscourt for the study of prophecy. To these meetings Mr. Darby and Mr. Billet were invited. Here also they met Mr. George V. Wigram, who was

to become one of Mr. Darby's most earnest collaborators in after years...Many other clergymen attended, and quite a few who were linked with the Irvingites.[12]

The Powerscourt meetings on prophecy started expressly for the purpose of popularizing the pre-tribulation rapture concept. Irving preached the pre-tribulation rapture in his own church and it became known as one of the distinctive tenets of his new Irvingite sect. It had taken Irving six years to dispose of his first English translation of Lacunza's book which he had finished in 1827. In 1833, Irving came out with a cheap popular edition of Lacunza's work, about the same time the Powerscourt meetings began.

Two things are of interest about the Powerscourt meetings. First, Darby and the other Brethren leaders, who as yet knew nothing of a secret rapture, had nothing to do with organizing the meetings. They were invited without being told about the pre-tribulation rapture agenda. Second, the Irvingites came to the meetings obsessed with the idea of the secret rapture. Following these meetings, Darby and other Brethren leaders zealously published the doctrine of the secret pre-tribulation rapture across the country. Regardless of theological differences, it is clear that Darby had accepted this Irvingite teaching.

The prophetic views emanating from Powerscourt Castle gained wide acceptance in several denominational circles, chiefly through the writings of such men as Darby, Bellet, Newton, S.P. Tregelles, Wigram and Andrew Junkes. William Kelly spread the word after 1845, whose name was linked with the movement; there was also C.H. Mackintosh, Charles Stanley, J.B. Stoney, Charles Scofield and others.[13]

Dr. S.P. Tregelles, an accomplished Greek scholar and editor of the Greek New Testament, was one prominent church leader who accepted the secret rapture doctrine during this period. He was probably the most learned man within Brethrenism, and surely his name was an asset to their cause. Sometime later he denounced this new concept. After further study, he gave a clear ringing testimony against it. He concluded:

> I am not aware that there was any definite teaching that there would be a secret rapture of the church at a secret coming, until this was given forth as an utterance in Mr. Irving's church, from what was there received as being the voice of the Spirit. But whether anyone ever asserted such a thing or not, it was from that supposed revelation that the modern doctrine and modern phraseology arose. It came not from Holy Scripture, but from that which falsely pretended to be the Spirit of God.

In summary, it was Emanuel Lacunza, alias Rabbi Ben Ezra, a Chilean Jesuit of Spanish descent, who first planted the seed of the pre-tribulation rapture doctrine. He introduced the concept in his book, *The Coming of the Messiah in Glory and Majesty,* first published in 1816. This book was translated into English by Edward Irving and published in 1827. Dr. Maitland, librarian to the Archbishop of Canterbury, and Edward Irving, for whom the Irvingites were named, then introduced this new prophetic concept to the British people. After 1833, Tractarianism and Brethrenism spread this teaching throughout Protestant Christianity.

SCRIPTURAL EVALUATION OF THE PRE-TRIBULATION RAPTURE

As we have seen, the pre-tribulation doctrine has a checkered history. But what does the Bible say? The Bible plainly records that a rapture or calling up of the saints will occur.

> For the Lord himself will come down from heaven, with a loud command, with the voice of the archangel and with

the trumpet call of God, and the dead in Christ will rise first. After that, we who are still alive and are left will be caught up together with them in the clouds to meet the Lord in the air. And so we will be with the Lord forever. (1Thessalonians 4:16-17)

The issue is *when* this will occur. Darby, taking his cue from Irving, taught that Jesus might return at any moment to raise the dead in Christ and translate believers. Then after the disappearance of the believers, the anti-Christ would openly reign over the whole world.

Besides Darby, Charles Scofield, who was closely associated with the teachings of both the Brethren and Darby, has probably done more than any single individual to propagate the pre-tribulation rapture teaching in the United States. Scofield incorporated this idea in notes adjacent to the text of Scripture in his Scofield Reference Bible. How many have read it and believed it thinking it was part of the inspired Word of God? I do not object to Mr. Scofield, or anyone else, adopting this prophetic theory. I consider Mr. Scofield a brother in full fellowship who has accomplished much. But I doubt whether I, Mr. Scofield, or anyone else should assume the right to record and print next to the text of Scripture in a formal Bible what can only be regarded as a doctrinal concept.

Darby and Scofield offered a "scriptural basis" for the pre-tribulation rapture doctrine. Many church members today refer to these same passages. Their interpretations include:

(1) The Worthy to Escape Doctrine
(2) The One Taken and One Left Doctrine
(3) The Man-Child Theory
(4) Enoch, Elijah, and Noah
(5) The Church and the Book of Revelation
(6) About Giving It to the Jewish People

(7) A New Dispensation Theory
(8) The Thessalonian Letter.

Judge for yourself whether or not the Bible indicates the pre-tribulation timing of the rapture.

The Worthy to Escape Doctrine

Two passages of Scripture, one from Luke and the other from Revelation, were favorite texts for Darby. In Luke, Darby read "Watch ye therefore, and pray always, that ye may be accounted worthy to escape all these things that shall come to pass, and to stand before the Son of Man" (Luke 21:36 KJV). He interpreted "things that shall come to pass" to mean persecutions under the anti-Christ, but is that what the Bible says? This verse appears to refer to end-time events, but nothing is said of an anti-Christ. Read Luke 21 to learn the context of this verse.

Darby took the "worthy to escape" phrase from the King James Version, the only version that was available to him. Recent translations provide a better understanding of the Greek and raise the question if Darby would infer the same thing today. For example, the Revised Standard Version renders this verse, "But watch at all times, praying that you may have strength to escape all these things that will take place, and to stand before the Son of Man" (Luke 21:36). This version reads "strength to escape," not "worthy to escape." The New American Standard version also reads "strength to escape." The New International version reads "able to escape." Why does Scripture say we are to be alert and pray for His strength if we are not going to be here in that period of time?

Another "worthy to escape" passage used by Darby states, "Because thou hast kept the word of my patience, I also will keep thee from the hour of temptation, which shall come upon all the world, to try them that dwell upon the earth" (Revelation 3:10 KJV). Darby and Scofield assumed, therefore taught, the "hour of temptation" would be that period of time in which the anti-Christ reigns. Being "kept from the hour of temptation" they said, meant being translated into heaven before that reign began.

But what does it mean to be "kept"? The Greek word used in this verse for "keep" is *tereo,* which carries the meaning "to watch over, preserve, hold fast, keep through" or "keep away from." It also means "protecting." How we are to be kept or protected is not stated, but one thing is certain. If anyone was ever worthy of escaping trials and tribulations, it is the Lord Jesus Christ. Yet He endured the suffering of the cross. He was not spared His hour of temptation. As His servants, are we better than our Master? Not according to John 15:18-20. God is able and willing to keep us through all trials, temptations and tribulations of this world (John 16:33, 1 John 4:4). I firmly believe Scripture teaches we will be kept through the hour of temptation. Jesus was, as were saints though the ages, but it was by God's power and grace which proved to be sufficient, not by escaping. Escaping does not allow God to show the world He has the real power. Christians in foreign lands (Corrie ten Boom, for example) have called our doctrine of the pre-tribulation rapture an American theology that puts the spiritual emphasis on protecting the flesh.

The One Taken and One Left Doctrine

Darby, and Scofield, used two verses from Matthew 24 to support their teaching on the pre-tribulation rapture doctrine. In verse 40, Jesus says that at the time of His return two would be grinding at the mill, one would be taken and the other left. In verse 41, he says that two would be together in the field; one would be taken and the other left. Darby taught the ones "taken" were the Christians during the pre-tribulation rapture.

The "one taken and the other left" concept as being a calling out of the saints before the tribulation can only be theoretical. In Matthew 13 beginning with verse 24, Jesus gives us a parable about the Kingdom.

> Another parable he [Jesus] put before them, saying, "The Kingdom of Heaven may be compared to a man who sowed good seed in his field; but while men were sleeping, his enemy came and sowed weeds among the wheat, and went away. So when the plants came up and bore grain, then the weeds appeared also. And the servants of the householder came and said to him, 'Sir, did you not sow good seed in your field? How then has it weeds?' He said to them, 'An enemy has done this.' The servants said to him, 'Then do you want us to go and gather them?' But he said, 'No; lest in gathering the weeds you root up the wheat along with them. Let both grow together until the harvest; and at harvest time I will tell the reapers, Gather the weeds first and bind them in bundles to be burned, but gather the wheat into my barn.'" (Matthew 13:24-30 RSV)

In verse 36 of the same chapter, Jesus begins to explain the parable.

> Then he left the crowds and went into the house. And his disciples came to him, saying, "Explain to us the parable of the weeds of the field." He answered, "He who sows the good seed is the Son of man; the field is the world, and the good seed means the sons of the kingdom; the weeds are the sons of the evil one, and the enemy who sowed them is the devil; the harvest is the close of the age [the world], and the reapers are angels. Just as the weeds are gathered and burned with fire, so will it be at the close of the age [the world]. The Son of man will send His angels, and they will gather out of his kingdom all causes of sin and all evildoers, and throw them into the furnace of fire; there men will weep and gnash their teeth.

Then the righteous will shine like the sun in the kingdom of their Father. He who has ears, let him hear." (Matthew 13:36-43 RSV)

These verses are inconsistent with the idea that when the Lord comes He will first gather the wheat (good seed or Christians) from among the weeds (people of the world). Jesus will first gather the "weeds," not the "wheat." Jesus will gather the "weeds" out of the "good seeds;" he will not leave the weeds behind but gather them into bundles to be "burned." This prophecy cannot be fulfilled by a pre-tribulation rapture. Christians will have to remain on the earth through the tribulation with the people of the world rather than being pulled out beforehand.

The Man-Child Theory

When Darby first took the secret rapture theory from the Irvingites, he used the twelfth chapter of Revelation for scriptural support. According to Darby, the "man-child in Revelation 12 is the raptured church." Darby initiated the idea of applying the man-child to the rapture doctrine. Read the first few verses of Revelation 12. See if your spirit does not agree that the woman spoken of refers to Israel and that her child, who is caught up to rule from the throne of God, describes our Lord Jesus Christ. Revelation 12:5 says, "She [Israel] gave birth to a son, a male child, who will rule all the nations with an iron scepter." Other scriptures support the same concept of Jesus' rule (Romans 15:12; Ephesians 1:20-22; Revelation 19:15).

Enoch, Elijah, Noah

Another teaching offered to support the new concept of a pre-tribulation rapture was based on principles displayed in the lives of Enoch, Elijah, and Noah. Enoch and Elijah, he said, symbolized a type of the secret pre-tribulation rapture of the church before the so-called great tribulation. Similarly, Noah and his family, saved from the flood, were types of Jews preserved through the great tribulation.

What, if anything, about the lives of Enoch and Elijah typifies the translation of the church? Elijah suffered much persecution during his life on the earth. No extended period of tribulation or time of persecution followed soon after the translation of either Enoch or Elijah; there was no great tribulation for these men to escape. Nor are there any Scriptures to indicate that the translation of Enoch and Elijah symbolizes the pre-tribulation rapture of the church. According to Scripture, these two men were translated to heaven without dying because of their close walk with God and their faithfulness. Is the church walking that close to God today?

As for the teaching that Noah typifies the salvation of the Jews through the great tribulation, the Bible plainly explains the meaning of Noah's salvation from the flood. From Peter 3:18-21, we understand that Noah's salvation typifies our salvation from the world by baptism accompanied by the right attitude of heart toward God. As Noah was saved from the destruction of the world, so will we be saved from its final destruction. Baptism relates to the use of water in Noah being saved from the destruction of the wicked.

> ... Not as a removal of dirt from the body but as an appeal to God for a clear conscience, through the resurrection of Jesus Christ, who has gone into heaven and is at the right hand of God, with angels, authorities, and powers subject to him. (1 Peter 3:21-22 RSV)

There are no Scriptures to suggest that the account of Noah is intended to teach anything about a pre-tribulation rapture of the church in the end-time before the tribulation. If there is a parallel to end-time events, it is that God's power safely kept Noah and his family, both during the flood and pre-flood period. This has been God's method all through the ages.

The Church and the Book of Revelation

Darby and his followers developed another thought from the book of Revelation. They reasoned that because the church is not specifically mentioned after the fourth chapter, nothing from the fourth chapter to the end of the book applies to the church. Scofield provided an additional reason. He concluded that the catching up of John from earth to heaven in Revelation 4:1-2 symbolized the rapture of the church before the events of the tribulation described in chapters 6 through 19. But Revelation 4:1 says of John, "Come up here, and I will show you what must take place after this." The reason John was lifted up was to show what was yet to take place. No mention is made of any connection to a concept that the church will be raptured.

Here are four reasons that challenge Darby's and Scofield's theory that the book of Revelation does not apply to the church. First, the word "church" is not mentioned many times throughout the New Testament although the writers were sending messages to all Christians (the church). Furthermore, because the word "church" is not specifically mentioned in other books has not been a reason that we do not apply the teaching in them to the entire church. Why apply this idea solely to the book of Revelation? Isn't that an instance of trying to bend scriptural interpretation to fit a preconceived notion?

Second, it is commonly believed that the "church" *(Ekklesia)* refers to all believers and constitutes all of the saints. Although the word "church" does not appear in many locations, the Scriptures are still talking about the entire church. In the New Testament, the word "believers" or "saints" is used in a manner that we today would often use the word "church." In the same way, there are "believers" and "saints" mentioned *throughout* the book of Revelation.

Third, to whom did John write the book of Revelation? If there is one book in the New Testament specifically directed toward the church (the Body of Christ), it is the book of Revelation. The first chapter reads, "John, to the seven churches in the province of Asia" (Revelation 1:4). If most of this book (chapters 4-22) did not apply to the churches, wouldn't John have explained this especially after clearly stating that it was directed *to the churches?*

Fourth, the book of Revelation begins by stating it is directed to the churches, and ends by stating, "I, Jesus, have sent my angel to give you this testimony for the churches" (Revelation 22:16). If most of the book does not involve the church, why does it begin and end with references to the church?

About Giving it to the Jewish People

Another passage of Scripture that squarely contradicts the pre-tribulation rapture theory reads:

> Immediately after the tribulation of those days the sun will be darkened, and the moon will not give its light, and the stars will fall from heaven, and the powers of the heavens will be shaken; then will appear the sign of the Son of man in heaven, and then all of the tribes of the earth will mourn, and they will see the Son of man coming on the clouds of heaven with power and great glory; and He will send out His angels with a loud trumpet call, and they will gather his elect from the four winds, from one end of heaven to the other. (Matthew 24:29-31 RSV)

How did Darby account for this passage that says "Immediately after the tribulation...then will appear the sign of the Son of man...and they will see the Son of man coming on the clouds of heaven?" He explained away these verses by saying that after the rapture of the church, during the tribulation period, the Lord would deal with the Jewish people in a special way. The Lord would lead them in the proclamation of the "gospel of the kingdom." Later, Darby enlarged this explanation to include a unique group of Gentiles he called "the tribulation saints." He said the Lord was speaking of a Jewish remnant and their converts when he spoke of His coming "immediately after the tribulation of those days." These verses, Darby said, do not concern the church.

Is this explanation consistent with Bible teaching about Israel? Revelation 7:9-14, which is also talking about the tribulation, indicates that a great multitude from "every" nation, tribe, people, and tongue will come out of the great tribulation; not just a Jewish remnant and their converts as Darby asserted.

Darby's concept of giving-it-to-the-Jews opened the door for a variety of theories over the last 150 years. Darby's teaching that after-tribulation signs concerning the Lord's return apply only to the Jewish people has prompted others to take his idea even further. Some have gone so far as to apply all of the Sermon on the Mount solely to the Jewish people. Others have given the whole gospel of Matthew to the Jewish people. Still others have sliced out other parts of the New Testament and made them an exclusively Jewish heritage. When Jesus taught His disciples about the signs of his return "immediately after the tribulation of those days," I believe He was talking about both Jewish and Gentile believers. If He meant otherwise, surely He would have been more clear in letting it be known because in Christ there is neither Jew or Greek (Galatians 3:28). He has made us one body (Ephesians 2:14-16).

A New Dispensation Theory

Neither Darby nor Scofield ever denied that believers appear throughout the events described in the book of

Revelation. Acknowledging these Revelation saints created an obvious problem: Who are the saints described
in Revelation if they are already raptured before the
period of tribulation began? Darby resolved this contradiction with the idea of a special dispensation between
the time the Lord comes to rapture the church and the
end of the age.

Accepting the "new dispensation" doctrine meant
believing the Lord would deal with Israel in a particular
way. According to Darby's "gospel of the kingdom," a different group of believers appear in Revelation called the
tribulation saints. If Darby is right in claiming the time he
called the great tribulation would also be a new dispensation, then it is also a time of the greatest revival. John
says of this time:

> After this I looked, and behold, a great multitude which
> no man could number, from every nation, from all tribes
> and peoples and tongues, standing before the throne and
> before the Lamb, clothed in white robes, with palm
> branches in their hands, and crying out with a loud voice,
> "Salvation belongs to our God who sits upon the throne,
> and to the Lamb!"... Then one of the elders addressed me,
> saying, "Who are these, clothed in white robes, and
> whence have they come?" I said to him, "Sir, you know."
> And he said to me, "These are they who have come out of
> the great tribulation; they have washed their robes and
> made them white in the blood of the Lamb." (Revelation
> 7:9-10, 13-14 RSV)

Although Darby and Scofield said that the white-robed
people are not the church, Revelation chapter seven
reads that great multitudes would be saved from every
nation, not just Israel as Darby asserted. The number
saved will be so great that "no man can number." Where
did they come from? Verses 13 and 14 say, "Out of the
great tribulation," when according to the pre-tribulation
rapture concept all Christians are gone, the Holy Spirit is

gone, and the great apostasy occurs. How can the revival John speaks of in Revelation seven occur if all of the Christians (the church) are gone and the Holy Spirit is gone as Darby asserted?

The Thessalonian Letter

Since the new doctrine of the pre-tribulation rapture contradicted many passages of Scripture, it became necessary to explain away these contradictions. To do this, Darby devised new interpretations. One passage that contradicts the idea of a pre-tribulation rapture is found in 2 Thessalonians 2:1-6:

> Now concerning the coming of our Lord Jesus Christ and our assembling to meet Him, we beg you, brethren, not to be quickly shaken in mind or excited, either by spirit or by word, or by letter purporting to be from us, to the effect that the day of Lord has come. Let no one deceive you in any way; for that day will not come, unless the rebellion comes first, and the man of lawlessness is revealed, the son of perdition, who opposes and exalts himself against every so-called god or object of worship, so that he takes his seat in the temple of God, proclaiming himself to be God. Do you not remember that when I was still with you I told you this? And you know what is restraining him now so that he may be revealed in his time. (RSV)

Although this Scripture clearly states the coming of Christ and the translation of the living believers will follow the rebellion (falling away) when the man of lawlessness is revealed, Darby stated that the "coming of our Lord Jesus Christ" in this Scripture was not the same as "the day of Christ." He also said that "the day of Christ" is not the same as "the day of the Lord." This explanation has been repeated so often that it now is stated as a fact, but it has no scriptural support. If Darby had compared all the Bible references to the "day of Jesus Christ," he would have found reason to accept 2 Thessalonians 2:1-6 for what it says.

Paul's warning in these verses calls for an even greater measure of caution. Paul explicitly tells us not to be deceived on this subject by a "spirit," by a letter, or by anyone, even if they claim to have Paul's own authority. If the timing of the Lord's return has nothing to do with the appearance of "the rebellion [falling away] and reign of lawlessness," why would Paul bother these Thessa-lonians? They were already confused on this subject, and by using language and terms that did not have an appar-ent meaning, Paul would only have added to their confu-sion. I think Paul's purpose in this writing was not to con-fuse the issue, but to make things clear to these Christians who had evidently accepted contrary teach-ings. Paul definitely says that no one is to believe a con-trary teaching about the time of the coming of Christ, even though it may come from someone who claims to have received a special revelation given by a "spirit." If we accept Darby's teaching that this portion of Thessalonians needs additional clarification, then we would have to conclude that Paul failed in his writing to the Thessalonians.

Another passage Darby used to support the pre-tribu-lation rapture came from verse six in 2 Thessalonians chapter 2. Paul, in this verse, says, "You know what is restraining him now [referring to the man of lawless-ness] so that he may be revealed in his time." It is a known fact the Holy Spirit overall restrains lawlessness. Darby declared that the Holy Spirit relies on the church as his restraining agent on earth, therefore, the church must be removed before the man of lawlessness can be revealed. In other words, "the church will be raptured before the man of lawlessness appears."

The Bible just does not teach that the church is God's only agent to restrain lawlessness, nor do I believe church history reveals that the church is God's main agent to restrain lawlessness. It is true that where the church is free to declare God's standards like here in America, then the church is obliged to protect people from lawlessness by influencing government to maintain the rule of law. But what restrained lawlessness before the Church Age? What about that part of the world that has mostly been without the church to this present day? If we take count, the church of Jesus Christ has had little, if any, noticeable influence on restraining lawlessness in most societies and governments in the greater part of the world. How about the former Soviet Union, China, India, Africa—entire countries and whole continents that the church has failed to reach? God's means of restraining lawlessness by allowing evil to continue to a point determined by His will has never been confined to the church of the New Testament. Satan is the prince of this world (Ephesians 2:2), the god of this world (2 Corinthians 4:4); he would have destroyed us long ago and claimed the earth for himself if it had not been for the restraining hand of God. He alone rules over all.

I believe the Scriptures point to another agency here on earth instituted by God to restrain lawlessness. Romans 13:1-7 indicates, and history confirms, that the agency ordained of God to hinder and restrain the spirit of lawlessness is government. In these verses, Paul is talking to Christians about the Roman government, a government that cruelly persecuted the early church. He states it was instituted by God to maintain law and order and to control lawlessness. He tells these Christians they were to obey and respect civil authority. This is the agency that God institutes throughout the world to restrain lawlessness today. The church is to be the light of the world and salt of the earth. It has little influence in many pagan countries, yet lawlessness is controlled more there than here in the United States. How? By government, ordained by God to control lawlessness which is according to Scripture.

Are saints better today than those of the early church? Or, are we too weak and cowardly in our present day to suffer tribulation and hence desire to be taken away lest we fail the Lord in the time of trial? Surely not. Shouldn't every follower of the crucified Christ be prepared to go through great tribulation to glory and leave it to our Lord Jesus to empower us to work it all out? I hope you are not afraid to act on these thoughts because they are contrary to your current understanding. If new understanding of Scripture leads us to new truth, then let that be the road we commit ourselves to, regardless of what it may involve in the way of pleasure or pain. The decision is yours. Pray and seek the Lord on these matters. And most important, be honest before the Lord in all your ways and you will find His source for victory.

TO BELIEVE OR NOT TO BELIEVE

Whether you choose to accept or reject the material presented, I want you to know we have complete unity to love in and through our Lord Jesus Christ. I do not fully comprehend the great power and love God has for me, but I know He will work it through me in a period of tribulation. This is what allowed Jesus to say, "In this world you will have trouble. But take heart! I have overcome the world" (John 16:33). Since I have yet to experience that kind of spiritual power, Jesus' promise is still beyond complete understanding. But if I look to Jesus and many other overcomers throughout history, I can know that they overcame not by being taken out of the world, but only through living victoriously through trials or tribulations. God is faithful. His power and love have never failed. His faithfulness is demonstrated to the world by giving His people victory through tribulation. That is how I believe so many will be saved from every tribe and nation in the great tribulation as stated by John in Revelation chapter seven. Jesus said,

> If the world hates you, know that it has hated me before it hated you. If you were of the world, the world would love its own; but because you are not of the world, but I chose you out of the world, therefore the world hates you. Remember the word that I said to you, "a servant is not greater than his master." If they persecuted me, they will persecute you; if they kept my word, they will keep yours also. (John 15:18-20 RSV)
>
> I have said all of this to you to keep you from falling away. They will put you out of the synagogues; indeed, the hour is coming when whoever kills you will think he is offering service to God. And they will do this because they have not known the Father, nor me. But I have said these things to you, that when their hour comes you may remember that I told you of them. (John 16:1-4 RSV)

I believe it is important to set forth some of the things that both history and the Bible reveal concerning this doctrine of the pre-tribulation rapture. I realize that whatever one's doctrinal stance on this subject it does not affect a person's salvation. However, I believe it might develop in us a desire to protect our flesh and thus affect our faith in a time which will require our total commitment. It appears to me the pre-tribulation rapture doctrine contributes to the current apathetic attitude.

The concept of the pre-tribulation rapture is not the way of the Old Testament prophets. It is not the way of the cross nor the way the church came down through the centuries.

H.A. Baker, author of *Through Tribulation*,[14] once believed the pre-tribulation rapture concept. But while working as a missionary at an orphanage in China, the Holy Spirit revealed to him that this doctrine was based on scriptural inference and not on definite statements of Scripture. The Lord confirmed this light to Baker by pouring out His Holy Spirit upon many orphans in his care. The children had repeated visions of the persecution of Christians (the church) during the reign of the anti-Christ spirit of Satan in the end times. Baker also reports that these same children had repeated visions of the preaching of the gospel with unusual power during this same time, confirming the Lord's faithfulness in tribulation.

I have presented this information on the pre-tribulation rapture so that if it does not come, as many now believe, and we enter into the tribulation period, you will remember what the Word of God has told us about these things, and your faith will remain strong and you will not fall.

Chapter 9

A CALL TO ARMS

The greatest battle Christians face is not against other human beings, but against spiritual forces. Paul writes: "For our struggle is not against flesh and blood, but against the rulers, against the authorities, against the powers of this dark world and against the spiritual forces of evil in the heavenly realms" (Ephesians 6:12). Battling an enemy that cannot be seen sounds strange. It's difficult to imagine, and perhaps a bit uncomfortable, to think about going up against intangible forces of evil. It sounds unreal because many churches do not provide adequate teaching on spiritual warfare.

Picture a soldier going into battle. Spiritual warfare is no more mysterious than that. A soldier must be fit, tough, and alert at all times. A soldier carries powerful weapons and knows how to use them. If he does not know how, his chances of getting hurt greatly increase. A soldier depends on training, preparation, and above all, leadership, to win the victory. The same is true of the committed Christian. This Christian knows the power of prayer, the necessity of being grounded in God's Word, and of the Holy Spirit's work. The committed Christian knows what to expect from Satan and how to resist him. The committed Christian relies on the leadership of Christ and Christ alone.

In this book I have shared the five major warnings the Lord has given me to help guide our family's Christian walk of holy fear in these troubled times.

(1) The revelation which identified the end-time beast system prophesied by John.

(2) The warning of many seducing spirits working through the beast system to deceive many people.

(3) How these seducing spirits have developed a condition of spiritual heart disease in our country.

(4) A warning of God's coming judgment of our spiritual ills.

(5) The role economics will play in carrying out this judgment.

Seek the Lord about the truth of these warnings. As you do the Lord will begin to develop a healthy *holy fear* in you that will enable you to become steadfast regardless of outside circumstances.

A major theme of this book is that something is terribly wrong in our nation and that there is something we can do about it. The majority of people in our country once had a fear of committing many of the sins people now feel free to commit. Many non-Christians had this fear as well. But that holy fear of the Lord has been lost in the last generation. It is one of the major consequences of the beast system's seduction and victimization of our people. Holy fear of the Lord brings *discernment* about *right* and *wrong*.

In this last chapter, I discuss how Christians can become soldiers in the spiritual war for the hearts and minds of the American people. For the Christian today, it's no use hoping to avoid active combat against Satan because we are right in the middle of the war. We are engaged in a spiritual war for America's Christian heritage and most Christians seem unaware. Christians must come to realize it's at a turning point. We must take up the weapons of commitment, deliverance, the Word of God, and prayer and fight the Enemy.

AT WAR WITH SATAN

No one likes to think about going into heavy spiritual combat, especially when other aspects of life appear to be just fine. Peace and prosperity is the ear-tickling message so popular today. It is so much easier to go to church for entertainment rather than to prepare for spiritual battle. Warfare is exhaustive, stressful, expensive— even dangerous at times. But our apathy about standing firm and living for righteousness must cease if true biblical standards are going to be preserved.

Knowing our Enemy

The Bible teaches that Satan is a powerful spiritual adversary, but not that Christians should live in fear of him. We *need to respect* the fact that he causes tremendous spiritual damage when we are not prepared to fight him. (Look at the downfall of several of Israel's leaders in the Old Testament, for example.) Christians must be warriors of the Lord. This is especially true here in America because our country has been the world's center of Christian teaching and activity during the last three hundred years of the Church Age. The ways of Satan, as presented in Scripture, reveal that he has reserved his fiercest onslaughts for America in these last days. He systematically removes as many biblical standards as he can, then moves in to pillage and destroy. If we are going to prevent him from tearing down our families and our nation along with them, we must fortify our means of resistance.

Sadly, the people of the world know the importance of understanding the competitor's tactics but Christians face the Enemy unprepared. Whether in business, military operations, sports, or even video games, worldly people carefully prepare themselves for defense and counterattack. Christians know very little about the tactics of the real enemy in these last days. Unfamiliar with the biblical principles of spiritual warfare, many Christians remain idle while Satan wages war on our society with terrifying success. The fact that humanism and New Age philosophy have taken over so many areas of our thinking and standards is just one of the Enemy's successful offensive strikes.

Satan is winning the war for the hearts and minds of Americans and many Christians do not know enough to be concerned. Many cannot recognize the Enemy's tactics, or what to expect from him. Those who have already been captured—and have surrendered many of their ideas and standards to the Evil One—do not know they have been victimized by spiritual deception. They often speak and act contrary to basic godly principles. This becomes all too obvious by the amount of Christian counseling today. Many pastors, in addition to scores of professional counseling organizations that have appeared in recent years, expend a large amount of their resources caring for needy Christians. Many contemporary Christians cannot overcome their problems because they do not see Satan and his worldly system at the root. Things continue to fall apart and these troubled Christians do not even know why.

Christians must become wise to Satan's battle plan in order to turn things around. Christian leaders can see the missiles coming. Air raid sirens can be heard by those who are listening. Some Christians are aware that we are involved in severe spiritual warfare for the control of the people in our nation. As more Christians become involved, the fury of battle will intensify. The Enemy is not going to let up because he knows his time is short. Satan is going to fight hard to the very end with all the strength he can muster. This means you and I need to know and understand what God's Word has to say about the way Satan conducts his end-time warfare. We need to be equipped with the Word so we can stave off his attack on our families and prevent other loved ones from the ravages of this spiritual holocaust.

Despite the many ministries that are devoted to Christian service, the dedication of numerous pastors and teachers, and the sacrifice and hard work of many Christians in other areas, the fruit produced by our society in recent years reveal that we are losing the spiritual war for America. We are fulfilling the prophetic word found in Revelation 13:7. This verse says: "It [the beast] was given power to make war against the saints and overcome them." Satan's beast-system has influenced and affected Christians spiritual walk to the point where many have lost sight of what it means to lead a committed spiritual life. We know what to say in Christian circles to make it seem as if we are devoted, but our actions broadcast our weakness to the world. I am not saying we lack the desire, but the proof of our lukewarm Christianity is plain to see. With all of the opportunities to grow in the knowledge of God available to us in America today, yet with the equally pervasive spirit of independence, self-gratification, and self-centeredness among God's people, what other conclusion can be reached?

You may not realize it, but God is allowing the church in America to be tested by our Enemy as never before. That is how the Lord determines our level of commitment to Him and His standards. *Satan is going to work through our system to the limits God will allow in his attempt to tear down our Christian heritage.* Count on it. This is why it is so critical today to answer the call to arms. Our heritage as a Christian nation will be lost forever if Christians do not make an effort to preserve God's standards of righteousness. The souls of our children and grandchildren are on the line.

A Call to Arms

It was never God's intention to draft a peacetime army. A peacetime army never wins any battles because it never takes to the battlefield. During a time of peace, soldiers spend all their time plotting battle plans, talking about when the enemy might attack, and going-through-the-motions of real warfare to keep up morale. Spiritually speaking, we are not living in a time of peace. So singing a few rousing choruses about being in the Army of God does not measure up. Acting as if Satan's attack were taking place in some far-away location will not do. Talking about our struggles as if we were engaged in spiritual combat but never really fighting is not acceptable.

As believers, we need to quit acting like a peacetime army. Material prosperity and leisure-oriented life styles have dulled our senses. Christians watch the moral decay of our society as if we were helpless and unequipped to change it. Just because we may not face what appears to be a personal crisis does not mean that Satan has called a cease fire. He takes prisoners every day. His purpose now is the same as it has always been: to steal, to kill, and to destroy (John 10:10). Only his tactics are different in today's battle plan as was prophesied. Through deception—seducing spirits—he has lulled us to sleep instead of attacking us head-on. Either way he will be able to neutralize our influence as long as we are not doing something to stop him.

God has never sounded retreat. God's people are not to flee from the Devil; he is supposed to flee from us (James 4:7). Think about it. We should be "taking prisoners", not the other way around. We should be liberating men and women from Satan's kingdom of darkness (Colossians 1:13). It's not a matter of enlisting or staying a civilian. Our Leader has not given us that choice. All Christians have already been drafted. There is not a single Christian who has not been called to become a soldier in God's army. There is no option. You can only be one of three things: a warrior, a deserter, or a POW. Satan welcomes deserters and POW's because they support his cause by their inactivity. Inactive Christians give aid and comfort to the Enemy.

We should be collecting our weapons for battle, not for a parade. Satan has declared war. We are in a war zone.

> Finally, be strong in the Lord and in his mighty power. Put on the full armor of God so that you can take your stand against the devil's schemes...Put on the full armor of God, so that when the day of evil comes, [it has arrived!] you may be able to stand your ground, and after you have done everything, to stand. Stand firm then, with the belt of truth buckled around your waist, with the breastplate of righteousness in place, and with your feet fitted with the readiness that comes from the gospel of peace. In addition to all this, take up the shield of faith, with which you can extinguish all the flaming arrows of the evil one. Take the helmet of salvation and the sword of the Spirit, which is the word of God. And pray in the Spirit on all occasions with all kinds of prayers and request. With this in mind, be alert and always keep on praying for all the saints. (Ephesians 6:10-18)

It is past time for born-again believers to take a stronger stand for God's standards. When we do not take this stand, we invite the world to question our love for God and our appreciation for the sacrifice Jesus made for our salvation. The lack of a clear stand also gives the world the freedom to challenge biblical standards. The testimony revealed through the lives of committed Christians demonstrating deep-seated attachment to biblical requirements is the only Christian message that will be heard *in this day when self-interest has replaced holy fear in so much teaching, and prosperity has replaced the cross in so much preaching.* It is time we show the world that it is our God, not the god of this world, who has the power. Our Commander-in-Chief is sovereign, not the world's leader.

The Turning Point

As I was thinking about the spiritual war for America, I remembered a dramatic turning point in this nation's Civil War. During the first few days of July, 1863, Union General George G. Meade's forces clashed with Robert E. Lee's Army of Northern Virginia at Gettysburg. Lee's defeat in that horrible slaughter broke the back of the Confederates, but celebration over the victory melted into disappointment when Meade failed to pursue Lee, and allowed his retreating army to cross the Potomac. President Lincoln never recovered from his disgust with Meade who had been content to halt the northern advance of Lee's army instead of seizing the opportunity to destroy it altogether. Later in that dreary autumn of 1863, with the graves still fresh, Lincoln journeyed to Gettysburg to dedicate the cemetery.

You have undoubtedly heard Lincoln's two-minute speech before, but look at it again from the perspective of the spiritual challenge to Americans:

> Fourscore and seven years ago, our fathers brought forth upon this continent a new nation, conceived in liberty, and dedicated to the proposition that all men are created equal. Now we are engaged in a great civil war, testing whether that nation, or any other nation, so conceived and so dedicated, can long endure. We are met on a great battlefield of that war. We are met to dedicate a portion of it as the final resting place of those who here gave their lives that this nation might live.
>
> It is altogether fitting and proper that we should do this, but in a large sense we cannot dedicate—we cannot consecrate—we cannot hallow this ground—the brave men, living and dead, who struggled here, have consecrated it far beyond our power to add or detract. The world will little note, nor long remember, what we

say here, but it can never forget what they did here. It is for us, the living, rather to be dedicated here to the unfinished work that they have thus far so nobly carried on. It is rather for us to be here dedicated to the great task remaining before us, that from these honored dead we take increased devotion to that cause for which they here gave the last full measure of devotion; that we here highly resolve that these dead shall not have died in vain; that this nation, under God, shall have a new birth of freedom, and that government of the people, by the people, and for the people, shall not perish from the earth.

Mr. Lincoln addressed the great concern of his day: that the tremendous sacrifices made by so many would not be in vain. He hoped that the principles on which this nation was founded, and for which these men had fought and died, would survive. Today we are in a great spiritual war to preserve the biblical principles that have historically anchored the American people. Many have gone before us and sacrificed much to preserve our spiritual heritage and you and I have reaped the benefits.

The downward slide of American society we have experienced in recent years is just beginning. We have already passed the point at which Christian standards have lost their influence over the every day affairs of the majority of Americans. Furthermore, many Christians have joined the "gimme generation" of greedy, self-centered Americans. But Christians cannot afford to follow the American Pied Piper's song of destruction. If the attitude among Christians about taking up their spiritual armor and becoming warriors for the Lord does not change—if Christians do not join the fight because they love God and His ways—then God's tremendous blessing on this nation will be lost.

THE WEAPONS OF SPIRITUAL WARFARE: COMMITMENT

How do we prepare for the purification of the church? How can individuals join the spiritual war against our Enemy? What can one person do about the collapsing political, moral, and economic foundations of this nation? These are profound questions. Rest assured there is a meaningful answer, but it cannot be laid out with a point-by-point program. We are dealing with a spiritual process that starts with the heart. Turning the tide in America's losing war with Satan must begin with individual commitment.

Individual Commitment

Before anything else can happen in our battle against the Enemy, we must repent of our apathy. "Sow for yourselves righteousness," Hosea 10:12 reads, "reap the fruit of unfailing love, and break up your unplowed ground; for it is time to seek the Lord, until He comes and showers righteousness on you." To become completely dependent upon the Lord; surviving the troubled days ahead begins and ends with this. Before the Lord can mobilize us for battle, we must be committed. In order to join those at the front lines, we must be committed. Commitment is prerequisite for spiritual warfare. No one should be spoiling for a fight with the Devil who has not first come to terms with his or her relationship to Jesus. The forces of evil cannot be defeated by lukewarm Christians. Spiritual warfare demands dedicated servants willing to put themselves and their interests aside in order to be used by God. According to scripture this is our reasonable service. Paul states:

> Therefore, I urge you brothers, in view of God's mercy [the Lord's rescuing us from eternity in hell] to offer your bodies as living sacrifices, holy and pleasing to God— this is your spiritual act of worship [reasonable service].

Do not conform any longer to the pattern of this world,
but be transformed by the renewing of your mind. Then
you will be able to test and approve what God's will is—
his good, pleasing and perfect will. (Romans 12: 1-2)

Spiritual warfare requires a greater level of commitment than most Christians in America seem willing to
make. The life styles of many Christians today reveal
their lack of sincerity. Too many Christians struggle with
the same problems that plague non-Christians. Many
more Christians have already admitted defeat. They
wash ashore at pastors' offices and Christian counseling
organizations seeking therapy. There is divorce, immorality, poor parent-child relationships, and dishonesty
among God's people. Nowhere in Scripture does it say it
has to be this way. In fact, the scriptural message says
just the opposite. We are to be the salt of the earth that
preserves good; a light set on a hill that offers hope to a
dark, sick world.

Commitment to the cause of Christ is not the same as
commitment to a church organization. Perhaps you have
already committed fully to a church organization and its
religious doctrine. Church membership, church atten-
dance, and church activities are valuable parts of the
Christian life; participating in a church community can
help give believers strength for spiritual victory over the
power of the inner sin nature. But commitment to a religious organization should not be confused with true
commitment to Jesus.

As Christians, it is Christ and Christ alone that is to be
the center of our lives. We must be sure to make Him and
His teachings the focus of our devotion, our dedication,
our worship. We must grow to become dependent on
Him alone in all things. Only then will the Living Word
come alive in our hearts and our actions. At many times
during the history of God's people, Christians had only
one thing: Jesus. They had no church buildings, no

radio/television ministries, no denominational outreaches. They only had Jesus. We talk about Jesus, we
sing to Jesus, some of us raise our hands to Jesus, so let
us be satisfied with only Him. Paul writes:

> He is before all things, and in him all things hold together.
> And he is the head of the body, the church; he is the begin-
> ning and the firstborn from among the dead, so that in every-
> thing he might have the supremacy. For God was pleased to
> have all his fullness dwell in him, and through him to rec-
> oncile to himself all things, whether things on earth or things
> in heaven, by making peace through his blood, shed on the
> cross. (Colossians 1:17-20)

Those who have given themselves up to Christ will
never be captured by the Enemy's forces. No casualties
will ever be taken among those who remain loyal to the
Lord. He promises it will go well with those who are
righteous (Isaiah 3:10) and that He will be a source of
strength to those who are willing to engage the Enemy
(Isaiah 28:5,6). He will fully equip us to carry out our
orders. We must take our position in God's Army, march
into spiritual warfare, and He will lead us to victory.

The world so desperately needs to see an army of dedicated Christians. We must begin to apply the soothing
power of the spiritual ointment God has given us to heal
society from the hurt and pain inflicted by the Enemy.
Let us prove the power of God in our lives by declaring
war against sin and starting a revolution for seeking
righteousness. We must show the world, by the fruits of
our lives, that we follow a more powerful God.
Christians bring disgrace and sadness to the kingdom of
God when non-Christians feel free to sin openly. This
society is in the shape it's in because the Christians
lights have gone out. As the line in the Christian song
says: "If we are supposed to be the light, why is everything so dark?"

The Heart

Whether or not you are prepared for battle all comes down to your heart. Every Christian needs to be careful about this because where the heart is concerned, there is a fine line between seeking Jesus and giving in to Satan. You see, many people of the world do not know any better than to behave as they do, but Christians should know better. Worldly people's minds are filled with the filth of American society, but Christians should keep their distance from this filth and not be overcome with evil. As Christians, accepting worldly thoughts as our standard is a sin. This kind of compromise opens the door for the Adversary to ravage a person's life, cause spiritual defeat, and stunt spiritual growth.

Christ should become the ruler of our hearts. Only then can the spiritual characteristics referred to as the Beatitudes become the inner workings of our lives. If we are to do battle in the spiritual realm, these characteristics must describe our heart. Although I defined these spiritual heart characteristics in chapter 5 when discussing spiritual heart disease, I want to review them here briefly because they are so important. Jesus teaches that a heart problem is the source of every life problem (Matthew 15:18-19).

According to Jesus, the general characteristics of the Christian are:

Poor in Spirit (Matthew 5:3). Poverty of spirit refers to the emptying of self-interest. It is a process in which our old sinful nature shrinks in order to make room for God's nature, His Holy Spirit. It is the key to everything that follows in the Christian walk.

Mourning (Matthew 5:4). This is to see the sin in ourselves for what it really is, and to see sin in the world for what it really is. It is to truly perceive what sin does to people—the pain, the sickness, the grief, the despair it causes—and how it grieves our Heavenly Father so deeply.

Meekness (Matthew 5:5). Meekness centers on our relationship to others and our response to events around us. Meekness does not mean weakness. It requires the submission of the will to God to arrive at a state of total dependence upon Him. Meek Christians recognize that they are vessels of God to be used for His purpose; they have put aside themselves—their "rights" and "needs".

Hunger and Thirst for Righteousness (Matthew 5:6). To the degree that we are emptied of self-interest, we will desire to be filled with God's righteousness. Then the Lord will turn that desire into a hunger and thirst that is never completely satisfied.

Merciful (Matthew 5:7). To have mercy means to have pity, compassion, and sorrow, but also, to act on these sentiments. The merciful Christian makes the proper distinction between the sin and the sinner.

Pure in Heart (Matthew 5:8). Purity of heart amounts to single-minded devotion to God. To truly know, glorify, love, and serve the King of Kings. A pure heart is free of hypocrisy.

Peacemaking (Matthew 5:9). God's greatest desire for His children is for them to be the instrument that brings about peace on earth and goodwill to men. Peacemakers concern themselves with bringing glory to God above all else. They view disputes, whether between individuals or nations, as distractions that detract from the glory of God.

Persecuted for Righteousness (Matthew 5:10). The world hated Jesus because of His ultimate goodness. So bright was His righteousness that it exposed the best efforts of those around Him as insincere, superficial, tasteless, and vain. His light had to be extinguished so the forces of darkness persecuted and killed him. Throughout history, Christians who have displayed the heart characteristics above have faced verbal and physical abuse.

The kind of commitment required for spiritual warfare deals squarely with the heart. These heart characteristics reveal to us that *being* is more important than *doing*. Actions or works should result from being.

Being a Christian soldier mandates close inspection of one's inner drives and motivations. Any Christian can do things outwardly to suggest deep-rooted spiritual commitment, but God cannot be fooled. True commitment to the Lord Jesus Christ is not of the flesh, but of the Spirit. It is of the heart. The Bible says, "That which is of the flesh is flesh, and that which is of the spirit is spirit" (John 3:6). No amount of human wisdom, emotion, or activity will do. Where is your heart? Can you pray the words of this song with the desire to make them wholly applicable to yourself?

> Change my heart, O God, Make it ever true.
>
> Change my heart, O God, May I be like you.
>
> You are the potter, I am the clay.
>
> Mold me and make me, This is what I pray.
>
> Change my heart, O God, Make it ever true.
>
> Change my heart, O God, May I be like you.

THE WEAPONS OF SPIRITUAL WARFARE: DELIVERANCE

When Christians do their part and reach individual commitment, then the Lord does His part and brings *deliverance.* The deliverance I am speaking of has to do with the greatest battleground of spiritual warfare a

Christian encounters. The warfare within! Deliverance deals with the power necessary to gain victory over the sin nature within our hearts. The committed Christian allows God to bring death to the old nature so that He can replace it with His new nature. Perhaps no other believer explains the struggle to be free from the inner sin nature as well as the Apostle Paul.

The Sin Principle

Paul teaches that only Jesus can really change us. He says: "Therefore, if anyone is in Christ, he is a new creature; the old has gone, the new has come!" (2 Corinthians 5:17). The Christian is a new being and Christ is the one who creates that new being. No religion, no church, no amount of personal willpower can bring about this radical character change. Religion can only change outward aspects of behavior, not the inner being. It is only when the believer's character is changed on the inside that true spiritual victory can be fully realized and the fruits of the Spirit become normal in the Christian life. Only Jesus can set the committed Christian free of the self-serving nature.

Paul had good reason to take pride in who he was in the natural man. He had religious training, political authority, economic status, educational accomplishment, and intellectual ability. Yet he discounted all these things. "All things which were gain to me," Paul proclaimed, "those I count lost for Christ; in fact I count everything loss that I might know Christ better" (see Philippians 3:7-8). What a testimony! Through his experience, he realized there is a single power that can deal with the influences and pressures of the world system. It is Jesus, only Jesus.

Like Paul, our overdeveloped flesh causes us to place great confidence in personal abilities, which leads us in turn to attempt to accomplish the things of God with human strength and human wisdom. As Christians, we seldom seem aware of choosing this path because most of us have not been freed from the power of the flesh. Too many Christians have not received deliverance from the ways of the natural man.

One of the major barriers to spiritual growth and maturing in Christ for Christians in this country has come about through society's (the beast-system's) ability to incite the desires of the flesh. The Christian community has never contended with such a powerful attack before. The electronic media has eroded this nation's moral foundation to the point that many Christians no longer possess a fear of sinning. Worldly standards have gained acceptance among Christians, and in many churches they have replaced biblical standards altogether. This kind of influence conditions Christians to respond to the desires of the old nature and step out of their walk with Christ. This overdevelopment of the flesh makes it extremely difficult to fulfill God's plan for His people to walk in the power of the Holy Spirit. Both Paul and John warn of this happening in the end-time church (2 Timothy 3:1-5; Revelation 13:7).

One of the first spiritual principles the Lord began to teach me after my brother Charles shared God's revelation with me about the identity of the beast, was that Christians are saved by grace through faith in the power and blood of Jesus. Because of this, each one of us can be at peace about the sins we have committed before God (Romans 5:1-11). But as we begin to live the Christian life, we soon discover that as we need forgiveness for our sins, we also need deliverance from who we are. An inner nature contrary to the will of God lurks within every Christian, and every Christian will find this nature leads them to sin. Each Christian must be delivered from a self-centered heart to live a victorious Christian life.

The principle of sin can dominate the Christian's nature regardless of how much one may study the Bible, pray, or attend church. Not that these things are unnecessary, they are crucial to living the Christian life. But it is wrong to trust them for victory over this inner sinful nature. As Christians, our deliverance is in Jesus Christ, the object of our reading, study, and prayer. These activities should help us realize our dependence on Him. Just as He saved us from our sins, we are dependent on His power to deliver us from the grasp of our inner nature that causes us to sin. We must place our trust in Christ alone.

In other words, before becoming a Christian it was only a question of the sins committed before God. As a Christian, the question becomes one of the sin principle working within each person. Christians who seek to do the will of God and read God's Word will discover that they need forgiveness for sin, but also need deliverance from the power rooted in their beings that leads them to sin. Although a Christian may desire in his or her mind to do the will of God and follow His commands, even the most sincere, committed Christian will discover that failure comes all too often.

Paul explained the process this way:

We know that the law is spiritual; but I am unspiritual, sold as a slave to sin. I do not understand what I do. For what I want to do I do not do, but what I hate I do. And if I do what I do not want to do, I agree that the law is good. As it is, it is no longer I myself who do it, but it is sin living in me. I know that nothing good lives in me, that is, in my sinful nature. For I have the desire to do what is good, but I cannot carry it out. For what I do is not the good I want to do; no, the evil I do not want to do—this I keep on doing. Now if I do what I do not want to do, it is no longer I who do it, but it is sin living in me that does it.

So I find this law at work: When I want to do good, evil is right there with me. For in my inner being I delight in God's law; but I see another law at work in the members of my body, waging war against the law of my mind and making me a prisoner of the law of sin at work within my members. What a wretched man I am! Who will rescue me from this body of death? Thanks be to God—through Jesus Christ our Lord!

So then, I myself in my mind am a slave to God's law, but in the sinful nature a slave to the law of sin.

Therefore, there is now no condemnation for those who are in Christ Jesus, because through Christ Jesus the law of the Spirit of life set me free from the law of sin and death. For what the law was powerless to do in that it was weakened by the sinful nature, God did by sending his own Son in the likeness of sinful man to be a sin offering. And so he condemned sin in sinful man, in order that the righteous requirements of the law might be fully met in us, who do not live according to the sinful nature but according to the Spirit. (Romans 7:14-8:4)

Paul learned that in the matter of forgiveness, we as Christians look to Christ and His atoning blood shed on the cross. In the matter of deliverance from the sin principle within our inner nature, we must look to Christ in our hearts. For forgiveness, we depend on what He *has done;* for deliverance, we depend on what He *will do* within us. Both forgiveness and deliverance flow from the same source—the Christian's unqualified dependence on Him alone. From start to finish He is the one who does it all. Christ is everything and everything is in Christ.

Paul had discovered his need for deliverance when he cried out, "what a wretched man I am" (Romans 7:21-25). As a Christian, he deplored his old, wicked nature and he asked the most important question: "Who will deliver me from this body?" (Romans 7:24). Up to this point he had relied on his own power to become Christlike. In his mind, he wanted to do what was right according to God's Word, but in his heart he knew how often he failed. He sought the Lord for deliverance, and when he did he found the answer: "Thanks be to God ...Through Jesus Christ our Lord!" (Romans 7:25). Paul received a revelation in his heart; just as he received forgiveness for his sins by believing in what the Lord Jesus had done, he could only receive deliverance from the power of his sin nature to the extent he allowed the Lord to complete this work within his heart.

What Deliverance Means

Deliverance from the power of our inner sin-nature requires a revelation of Christ in our hearts, not just an awareness in our minds of the sin principle. We must pray and seek God to make this truth part of us—not just an experience we have or something we are knowledge-able about—but part of our changed-nature. Paul says:

> I do not cease to give thanks for you, remembering you in my prayers, that the God of our Lord Jesus Christ, the Father of glory, may give you a spirit of wisdom and of revelation in the knowledge of Him, having the eyes of your hearts enlightened...That according to the riches of his glory he may grant you to be strengthened with might through his Spirit in the inner man, and that Christ may dwell in your hearts through faith; that you, being rooted and grounded in love, may have power to comprehend with all the saints what is the breadth and length and height and depth, and to know the love of Christ which surpasses knowledge, that you may be filled with all the fullness of God. (Ephesians 1:16-18, 3:16-19 RSV)
>
> It is no longer I who live, but Christ who lives in me; and the life I now live in the flesh I live by faith in the Son of God, who loved me and gave himself for me. (Galatians 2:20 RSV)

In my own life I have found this to be true. When the gospel of Jesus Christ first shone into my heart, I cried out for forgiveness. But as I began to grow in my Christian walk, I discovered the very same sin principle that plagued Paul was at work within me as well. There is a sin principle within me that is contrary to the heart of God; sin is the principle of my old nature. I began to realize more and more that not only had I committed sins before God, but that there was something terribly wrong inside myself. Regardless of how hard I tried not to be self-centered, not to fight for my rights, not get angry, not get caught up in things of the world, I failed.

It was the Word of God that revealed to me that I still have the nature of a sinner. There is within me, as there is in every human being, an inclination to sin; not because in my mind I want to be that way, but as Paul states, it is because of "the law of sin at work within my members" (Romans 7:23). As I search my heart (as the Word tells me I should), I find that I am not always truthful, loving, kind, selfless, devoid of pride, patient, obedient, longsuffering, and compassionate. I do not always display the heart characteristics Jesus said his followers should have. I need *forgiveness* for what I have done, and I need *deliverance* from what I am.

In Watchman Nee's *The Normal Christian Life,* he discusses the principles of deliverance from the power of the inner sin nature in great detail. Nee points out that we are prone to try to accomplish the things of God within our own strength, wisdom and abilities. And most often, we do not know this is our path because we have not been broken from what we are in the natural man — the flesh. It is as we surrender our inner will power and become poor in the spirit that the heart characteristics of God will become a greater reality in Christians lives. Deliverance is not a matter of willpower, of trying to do our best for God. It's a matter of *will* and *power:* we surrender our will, Jesus provides the power.

There should be more Christian teaching about the biblical principle of the need for deliverance from the inner sin nature because the world's influence is so strong today. The spirit at work in the world environment of the end-time church under the beast-system is a spirit which causes man to develop the soul-life, the abilities, ways of thinking, and skills of the natural man which are controlled by the sinful nature. The Bible says that this will not be a known condition in the church by the vast majority of Christians in these last days; therefore many will be deceived and conquered by the spiritual force of the beast (Revelation 13:7). The word "conquered" is not referring to salvation, but to our walking in victory over our sin nature through the power of the Holy Spirit. Our being *wholly dependent* upon the Lord, submitting to His will and His working within us— laying aside all of our natural abilities and skills—trusting in Him only. That is not the spiritual walk for most of us, though God desires that it would be. It has been through the temptations of the beast-system that Christians have become so independent and self-sufficient.

Deliverance will be difficult to accomplish because of the world's influence. The spiritual process of this happening is not easy because we live with the influence of the self- gratifying atmosphere of our society. In fact, our first reaction will probably be to try and accomplish the breaking of our will solely through our own willpower. This will never succeed because *the self will never crucify self.* As we turn everything over to God and become completely dependent on Him, by faith we can trust that He will develop that process and perform that work in our inner lives to change our hearts. Spiritual deliverance and surrender will result. His work may be quite different for each of us but the results will be the same. We will stand stronger with the power of Christ to overcome the spiritual influences of the Evil one who controls society

(1 John 5:19) and we will experience victories for the Lord in our lives as we do battle.

Do not be discouraged if you have tried to bring about a change in your spiritual life by yourself and failed to do so. Trying to heal oneself spiritually is a formula for the impossible. We lack the knowledge of our true inner being to heal ourselves. Our responsibility is to submit ourselves to the Lord, resist the Enemy through prayer, grow in our understanding of God's principles as found in the Word, and avoid the world's entrapments. But just as the Lord brought spiritual rebirth when we first submitted our heart to Jesus, He will bring us to spiritual maturity as soldiers equipped and prepared to fight the battles and be victorious, but it will only be as we submit our inner fleshly selfwill.

Satan devised the most deceptive red herring he could through the power of our society to tempt the desires of the flesh to erode the total commitment of the surrendered Christian. Satan's aim is to destroy that kind of heartfelt attitude and the realization of God's beautiful love it can bring to us. Christ alone provides security. We must unconditionally surrender to Him. He has rescued us from the effect of sin and set us free from the power of the world. "Whoever the Son has set free is free indeed" (John 8:36). Pray for God to give you a revelation in your heart that you may know and believe His truth. Just as Jesus conquered (overcame) the world, we can overcome the influence of the world through His power. In these last days where evil abounds and demons rage, a heart with an open door to the fullness of Jesus is our only hope.*

*I recommend you also obtain a copy of David Wilkerson's article on deliverance titled, *Sin Shall Not Have Dominion Over You* (Romans 6:14) dated May 1, 1992. Send your request to: World Challenge, P.O. Box 260, Lindale, TX 75771. Phone 903-963-8626.

THE WEAPONS OF SPIRITUAL WARFARE:
GOD'S WORD

Deliverance is not taught as much as it should be taught. Reading the Bible, however, is a more obvious part of the Christian life. Even though reading the Word of God is so obvious, it should be emphasized for the importance it has. Many scriptures attest to how important a weapon the Word of God is in spiritual warfare. So I will let the Bible speak for itself:

The Word of God is our defensive weapon. "The sword of the Spirit, which is the word of God" (Ephesians 6:17). "All Scripture is God-breathed and is useful for teaching, rebuking, correcting and training in righteousness, so that the man of God may be thoroughly equipped for every good work" (2 Timothy 3:16-17). "For the word of God is living and active. Sharper than any double-edged sword, it penetrates even to dividing soul and spirit, joints and marrow; it judges the thoughts and attitudes of the heart" (Hebrews 4:12). "Your word is a lamp to my feet and a light for my path" (Psalm 119:105). "The entrance of your words give light; it gives understanding to the simple" (Psalm 119:130).

The Word of God is to be written on our hearts. "Fix these words of mine in your hearts and minds; tie them as symbols on your hands and bind them on your foreheads. Teach them to your children, talking about them when you sit at home and when you walk along the road, when you lie down and when you get up" (Deuteronomy 11:18-19). "I have hidden your word in my heart that I might not sin against you" (Psalm 119:11).

The Word of God purifies life. "How can a young man keep his way pure? By living according to your word" (Psalm 119:9). "You are already clean because of the word I have spoken to you "(John 15:3).

The Word of God was written for a purpose. "For everything that was written in the past was written to teach us, so that through endurance and the encouragement of the Scriptures we might have hope" (Romans 15:4). "I write these things to you who believe in the name of the Son of God so that you may know that you have eternal life" (1 John 5:13).

The Word of God is absolutely trustworthy. "It is to be with him, and he is to read it all the days of his life so that he may learn to revere the Lord his God and follow carefully all the words of this law and these decrees" (Deuteronomy 17:19). "Now the Bereans were of more noble character than the Thessalonians, for they received the message with great eagerness and examined the Scriptures every day to see if what Paul said was true" (Acts 17:11). "The works of his hands are faithful and just; all his precepts are trustworthy" (Psalm 111:7). "Heaven and earth will pass away, but my words will never pass away" (Luke 21:33). "The law of the Lord is perfect, reviving the soul. The statutes of the Lord are trustworthy, making wise the simple" (Psalm 19:7).

To ignore the Word of God is perilous and foolish. "Jesus replied, 'You are in error because you do not know the Scriptures or the power of God'" (Matthew 22:29). "For we were born only yesterday and know nothing, and our days on earth are but a shadow" (Job 8:9). "I thought, 'These are only the poor; they are foolish, for they do not know the way of the Lord, the requirements of their God'" (Jeremiah 5:4). "My people are fools; they do not know me. They are senseless children; they have no understanding" (Jeremiah 4:22). "Even the stork in the sky knows her appointed seasons, and the dove, the swift and the thrush observe the time of their migration. But my people do not know the requirements of the Lord" (Jeremiah 8:7). "Furthermore, since they did not think it worthwhile to retain the knowledge of God, he gave them over to a depraved mind, to do what ought not to be done" (Romans 1:28).

THE WEAPONS OF SPIRITUAL WARFARE: PRAYER

Prayer, like Bible reading, seems rather obvious. Volumes have been written about prayer. There are several organizations across the country that conduct seminars on prayer. There are many aspects to prayer such as praise, thanksgiving, petitioning for our needs, submitting ourselves in commitment and dependence, spiritual warfare and more. Praying seems like such an easy thing to do. Perhaps it even seems meaningless to some to pray. But prayer is a major weapon in spiritual warfare.

The Lord has given the *weapon of prayer* to every Christian. It is an offensive weapon each of us must use to win over Satan. Christians attain power and boldness to do battle through prayer. It is the means by which we petition our needs before God. It is how we speak God's Word of Truth to our enemy declaring Jesus' victory over the rulers, authorities, powers and spiritual forces of evil. Revelation 12:11 states: "They overcame him by the blood of the Lamb and by the word of their testimony; they did not love their lives so much as to shrink from death." This verse contains the secret of victory of warfare. Personalize this verse.

"I overcame him (Satan and all his demons) by the blood of the Lamb (the atoning power of the blood of Jesus shed on the cross) and by the word of my testimony (speak out loud directly to the rulers and authorities of evil—Satan and his demons—by the authority and power given me in the name of Jesus); I do not love my life so much as to shrink from death (I will not hold back from entering into spiritual warfare because I love my life so much I am afraid of the consequences)."

Praying may seem too easy. It is in a way. Talking to our Heavenly Father is something any Christian can do. But it was not easy for Jesus. It cost Him His life. We should not be negligent about claiming what he purchased for us at so great a price. "Submit yourselves, then, to God. Resist the devil, and he will flee from you" (James 4:7). Prayer is a powerful weapon. Not to recognize the power means we do not understand the atonement of Jesus' death on the cross. Jesus was victorious. He overcame the enemy and all his demons. Through the name and blood of Jesus, that power which gives us victory is made available to us.

Prayer works. In the area of spiritual warfare, we can pray believing God will give us what we ask because God's Word states that Satan was defeated by the blood of Jesus. We can declare—through our testimonies—to all demons in hell that our Commander-in-Chief—Jesus—defeated their leader—Satan. Jesus' atonement for our sins gives us the right to speak directly to demons, to pull down dark strongholds, to drive away evil spirits. "For the weapons of our warfare are not carnal, but mighty through God to the pulling down of strongholds" (2 Corinthians 10:4 KJV). Christians can attack Satan's forces with the authority of the name of Jesus. We can approach the throne of God boldly—not in a position of power ourselves, but resting on the authority of Jesus Christ (Hebrews 4:16). Remember this: the power of the blood of Jesus that He shed at Calvary had the power to purchase our salvation and it has the power to gain victory for us in spiritual warfare. Each of us can wage spiritual war against the gates of hell by praying for our children, grandchildren, family, church, Christian organization and workers, city, nation, and leaders.

Now sometimes you will find that the Devil will not leave. No matter how often and how earnestly you pray Satan still seems to have power over an area of your life. He lingers because he has something on you. If your heart is not right before the Lord, if you have held anything back from God, if you still seek to take part of the world and its ways, Satan can gain a foothold. Spiritual warfare is one of the most powerful incentives for holiness. We cannot fight the Devil and live in sin. We cannot be Christ's by *profession*—yet the Devil's by *practice.* To follow Christ you must turn your back on the standards of the world. Christians must renounce sin and not yield ground (James 5:13-18).

Perhaps you are one of those Christians who have thought, "God already knows my needs, so why should I pray about them?" We need to understand that God has limited Himself to work in certain ways. For example, God will not preach the Gospel to anyone. This can be seen in His call to Peter to reach Cornelius. Prayer fits into this same category. God does not pray to Himself. He has told us to pray. We are charged with releasing His power through prayer. Every time we pray against the principalities and rulers of this dark world, we release God's power on earth. God will give us the victory—He said it belongs to us—but we have to ask for it.

So why don't we pray more than we do? Is it really because we do not have time? Or, is it because we're not really convinced of the power of prayer? If you are like many other Christians, you feel you are too busy to pray. So many things in life distract us from praying. But we must simply take time. We are ignorant of the power of prayer. Because of our ignorance we are reluctant to attack the Enemy. Therefore, Satan has deceived many Christians and dominates many aspects of their life styles. Remember this principle from Exodus 14: *You can do more than pray after you've prayed; you cannot do more until you have prayed.*

A LESSON FROM EXODUS

There is a lesson found in Exodus that speaks directly to our situation. A lesson for Christians living in the last days in America when a sober accounting of the present seems so troubling, and the future is even more desperate. Paul said, speaking of Old Testament events, "These things happened to them as examples and were written down as warnings for us" (1 Corinthians 10:11).

Exodus begins with the Israelites held captive by Pharaoh in Egypt. To understand the lesson for Christians today it is necessary to see aspects of the story have modern equivalents: Egypt represents the world, Pharaoh represents Satan, and the Israelites represent us. The Israelites were God's people on earth then, today God's people make up the church. Think about the parallel. There the Israelites were, trapped in Egypt. Egypt was the mightiest civilization on the earth. The Egyptians must have seemed overwhelming to the Israelites who were surrounded on all sides by Egyptian culture, technology, language, and religion. This is just as American society seems to Christians today—so pervasive, so powerful, so unavoidable. And there was Pharaoh. Pharaoh stood at the top of Egyptian civilization. He was the supreme leader. What was in the mind of Pharaoh became national policy. The same is true of Satan today. Satan is the ruler of this world and what is in the mind of Satan becomes the principles of worldly existence.

Notice that the Israelites were not enslaved because the Egyptians actually *were* stronger but because the Israelites *believed* the Egyptians were stronger. In fact, the Israelites were numerically superior to the Egyptians. Exodus 1:7 says, "The Israelites were fruitful and multiplied greatly and became exceedingly numerous, so that the land was filled with them." The Israelites outnumbered the Egyptians yet Pharaoh controlled them. More than anything else, Pharaoh feared the Israelites would discover that they were mightier than the Egyptians and revolt. This is Satan's fear today—that Christians will discover they are mighty in Christ. Satan knows we are stronger than he is, but most of us do not really know this. We may know it intellectually, but not really. We do not believe it deeply enough to take the fight to him. We are duped just like the Israelites.

Because Pharaoh could not overpower the Israelites, he knew that he would have to outsmart them. If the Egyptians were to keep the upper hand, Pharaoh realized it would have to be done by deceit rather than brute force. Exodus 1:9-10 reads: "'Look,' he [Pharaoh] said to his people, 'the Israelites have become much too numerous for us. Come, we must deal shrewdly with them or they will become even more numerous and, if war breaks out, will join our enemies, fight against us and leave the country.'"

How similar this is to Satan's method of bullying the church in America today. Our Christian community has been responsible historically for the greatest percentage of mission and Gospel outreach to the rest of the world. America was founded upon biblical principles. The United States started out as a Christian nation. Satan had never faced such a threat before. So rather than persecute American Christians outrightly as he did the early church, he turned to deception. He set the beast-system in motion and pulled out all the stops. Satan deceives us. He had to deal with us cleverly in order to place us in bondage to the world's influence. In this way he destroys many of the biblical standards followed by the people in our nation. His plan is working. Many of God's people have ceased to influence the world for good; rather, the world influences Christians for the bad.

It worked then too. Pharaoh fooled the Israelites into serving him. Exodus 1:11 states that the Egyptians, "put slave masters over them [the Israelites] to oppress them with forced labor, and they built Pithom and Rameses as store cities for Pharaoh." This is the saddest truth found in Exodus Chapter One. Rather than using their numerical strength to wrest free from Pharaoh's grasp, Pharaoh exploited the Israelites ignorance to make his regime stronger. The Israelites contributed to their own oppression and Pharaoh tightened the screws. He "made their lives bitter with hard labor in brick and mortar and with all kinds of work in the fields; in all their hard labor the Egyptians used them ruthlessly" (Exodus 1:14).

Just as Pharaoh oppressed the Israelites, Satan oppresses us. *Deception always brings domination.* Not necessarily physical oppression but emotional and spiritual oppression. Satan has tricked Christians into supporting worldly standards and accepting the world's philosophy of life. They no longer take their spiritual position in Jesus Christ and fight. He has trapped them into the joylessness of self-centered pursuits. Satan's tricks have sidelined many Christians and we are living with the results. Broken, wounded people fill church pews Sunday after Sunday. Families are falling apart, young people are doing themselves in, church leaders are giving up. The Enemy has stripped everything of value from us, yet many continue to help him do it. Satan cannot take away our salvation, but he can steal the inner peace and joy that belongs to us in Christ. He can get us to trade the victorious Christian life for an empty day-to-day existence not worth living.

By the end of Exodus 2, the Israelites are so worn out from their enslavement they cry out for God's help. Exodus 2:24 says that God heard their prayers. The next 38 chapters of Exodus tell about the miraculous exit of the Israelites from Egypt. They had no army, no allies, no supplies, yet three million of them walked away from the mightiest empire on earth. There is power is prayer! That same power is available today!

Are you tired of living in defeat? Tired of being exploited by Satan? Tired of believing the lies spread by this world system? Are you ready to stand and fight? Search out any area of your life that may give ground to the Enemy. Repent and receive God's forgiveness. Reclaim lost ground through praying in the authority of the name and the power of Jesus blood. There has never been a great move of God without prayer. So seize the opportunity. Take your needs to the Lord in prayer. Intercede for others. Then go out and do what God guides you to do. Prayer without action is a contradiction (Acts 4:29-31).

COURAGE THROUGH FEAR

It was my brother's revelation in 1971 that helped Barbara and me to understand the spiritual principles behind *how* and *why* Satan attacks society today. We believed God's revelation, and through our obedience in doing something about it, we have been able to avoid many of our society's spiritual pitfalls that have lured so many Christians, and caused them hard spiritual defeats and pain in their lives and the lives of their families.

Barbara and I developed holy fear as a consequence of this revelation and over the past 20 plus years, we have grown in this characteristic. We resolved to set our course of action for the saving of our family. This was done by completely committing ourselves to the ways of the Lord. It was from this revelation of God's Word concerning the end-time beast-system that came the backbone, the foresight and the key to unlock the Lord's wisdom for us to understand the attack Satan is using against God's people during these last days. The courage to follow the Lord came from holy fear.

Many of the causes of deteriorating morals in our society are what Barbara and I were warned about over 20 years ago. Many things we can plainly see today confirm this revelation. These are things that *we did not have the advantage of knowing then.* I believe it is because of this revelation, we were inspired through holy fear to build a spiritual ark for the saving of our family. All of our children, our own three and the six we added, are dedicated to serving the Lord. It inspired us to make our lives a positive influence on the lives of our family members. I close with a quote from Scripture.

> Blessed is the man who fears the Lord, who finds great delight in his commands ... Even in darkness light dawns for the upright, for the gracious and compassionate and righteous man. Good will come to him who is generous and lends freely, who conducts his affairs with justice. Surely he will never be shaken; a righteous man will be remembered forever. He will have no fear of bad news; his heart is steadfast, trusting in the Lord. His heart is secure, he will have no fear; in the end he will look in triumph on his foes. He has scattered abroad his gifts to the poor, his righteousness endures forever; his horn will be lifted high in honor. (Psalm 112:1,4-9)

FOOTNOTES

Chapter One

1. Robert W. Sweet, "Missing Children: Found Facts,"
   NIJ Reports, no. 222 (November /December, 1990),
   pp. 15-17.

2. *Sourcebook of Criminal Justice Statistics, 1990*
   (Bureau of Justice Statistics, Washington, DC: U.S.
   Government Printing Office, 1991) p. 387.

3. *Law Enforcement News,* volume 17, (September 15,
   1991), p. 3.

4. *Law Enforcement News,* volume 16 (September 15,
   1990), p. 3; volume 17, (July/August, 1991), p. 2.

5. *BJS Data Report, 1989,* (Rockville, MD: Bureau of
   Justice Statistics, 1990), p. 42; *Law Enforcement
   News,* volume 17, (March 31, 1991), p. 2; (April 30,
   1991), p. 2.

6. *Law Enforcement News,* volume 17 (June 15/30, 1991),
   p. 3.

7. *Sourcebook of Criminal Justice Statistics, 1989*
   (Washington, DC: Bureau of Justice Statistics, 1990)
   pp. 277-278.

8. *Law Enforcement News,* volume 17 (March 31, 1991),
   p. 2; (July/August, 1991), p. 3.

9. Words and music by Keith Green. © 1980 Birdwing
   Music/Cherry Lane Music Publishing Co., Inc.
   (ASCAP) (Div. of Sparrow Corporation, Chatsworth,
   CA 91311).

Chapter Three

1. Gordon W. Prange, *At Dawn We Slept* (New York:
   Penguin Books, 1982)

Chapter Four

1. Faith Campbell, *Stanley Frodsham: Prophet With A
   Pen* (Springfield, MO: Gospel Publishing House,
   1974).

2. National Institute of Mental Health, *Television and Behavior: Ten Years of Scientific Progress and Implications for the Eighties* (Washington, DC: U.S. Government Printing Office, 1982).

Chapter Five

1. See Watchman Nee, *Love Not the World* (Wheaton, IL: Tyndale House, 1988), pp. 11-13.
2. Nee, *Love Not the World,* p. 14.
3. James Dobson and Gary L. Bauer, *Children at Risk* (Dallas: Word Publishing, 1990).

Chapter Six

1. Pat Robertson, "Prepare for Economic Collapse," *End Times News Digest* 158 (November, 1991), p. 4.

Chapter Seven

1. Letter from David Wilkerson, 9 November 1987.
2. Pat Robertson, "Prepare for Economic Collapse," *End Times News Digest* 158 (November, 1991), p. 2.
3. Robertson, "Prepare for Economic," p. 1.
4. Robertson, "Prepare for Economic," p. 3.
5. *Los Angeles Times,* 25 August 1974.
6. *Wall Street Journal,* 11 November 1981.

Chapter Eight

1. Bob Summers, *Out Back With Jesus* (Fort Worth, TX: Harvest Press, 1975), pp. 4-8.
2. A detailed explanation of this point is not necessary because it is substantiated by a host of historical volumes. See Kenneth Latourette, *The History of Christianity* (New York: Harper and Row, 1953); Reinhold Seebert, *History of Doctrines,* volume 1, (Grand Rapids, MI: Baker Book House, 1966); Philip

Schaff, *History of the Christian Church* (Grand Rapids, MI: Eerdmans Publishing Co., 1910); Henry Bettenson, *Documents of the Christian Church* (New York: Oxford University Press, 1947); Hans Leitzman, *History of the Early Church* (New York: World Publishing, 1953); Arthur McGiffert, *A History of Christian Thought* (New York: Charles Scribner, 1933).

3. Duncan M. McDougall, *The Rapture of the Saints* (Blackwood, NJ: O.F.P.M Publishers, 1970).

4. Juan Josafat Ben Ezra [Emanuel Lacunza], *The Coming of Messiah in Glory and Majesty* (Dublin, Ireland: Wm. Curry Jon. and Co., 1833), pp. 10-11.

5. LeRoy Froom, *Prophetic Faith of Our Fathers,* volume 3, (1946), pp. 303-324.

6. Froom, *Prophetic Faith,* volume 2, p. 657; Guiness, *History Unveiling Prophecy,* (1905), pp. 285-289.

7. Froom, *Prophetic Faith,* volume 3, pp. 514-526; volume 4, pp. 420-422; Guiness, *History Unveiling Prophecy,* p. 240; Elliott, *Hoare,* volume 4, p. 552.

8. "Plymouth Brethren," *Encyclopedia Brittanica,* 11th ed., volume 21, p. 864.

9. Froom, *Prophetic Faith,* volume 4, p. 1223 – Note 6.

10. Harry Ironside, "A Historical Sketch of the Brethren Movement," *Serving and Waiting Magazine,* Philadelphia School of the Bible, (1925), p. 10.

11. Froom, *Prophetic Faith,* volume 4, pp. 1223-1225 and footnotes.

12. Ironside, "A Historical Sketch," p. 23.

13. Ironside, "A Historical Sketch," p. 23.

14 H.A. Baker, *Through Tribulation,* (Minneapolis, MN: Calvary Books and Tracts, N.D.).

ORDER FORM

For additional copies of HOLY FEAR use this page.
Please send me _____ copies of HOLY FEAR
@ $7.95 each.

Other important biblical principles about living the Christian life in America during these last days are shared in Bob Fraley's book, THE LAST DAYS IN AMERICA.

Please send me _____ copies of THE LAST DAYS IN AMERICA @ $7.95 each.

_____ copies of HOLY FEAR x $7.95 = $ _____

_____ copies of THE LAST DAYS
              IN AMERICA x $7.95 = $ _____

                    Handling & Postage $ ___ $2.00*

                              TOTAL $ _____

*Total charge for handling and postage regardless of quantity ordered.

Your Name: _____

Address: _____

_____

Mail this order form and check, cash or money order to:
Christian Life Outreach
6438 E. Jenan Drive
Scottsdale, Arizona 85254

Phone orders call (602) 998-4136

Please Note: All net proceeds from the sale of these books are used to help the poor and needy.